GROUND COVER
AND OTHER WAYS TO
WEED-FREE GARDENS

GROUND COVER AND OTHER WAYS TO WEED-FREE GARDENS

FREDERICK A. BODDY

DAVID & CHARLES
NEWTON ABBOT   LONDON   VANCOUVER

To my two sons, Christopher and Dennis,
who in their different ways have followed
in my footsteps.

0 7153 6575 4

© Frederick A. Boddy 1974

Set in 11 on 13pt Garamond and printed in
Great Britain by Latimer Trend & Company Ltd Plymouth
for David & Charles (Holdings) Limited
South Devon House   Newton Abbot   Devon

Published in Canada
by Douglas David & Charles Limited
3645 McKechnie Drive   West Vancouver BC

CONTENTS

LIST OF ILLUSTRATIONS

7

PUBLISHER'S PREFACE

Weeds spoil the enjoyment of many private gardens, the fulfilment of expectations in many commercial ones. Yet avoiding, controlling and even killing them can be absorbing and enjoyable. The professional is always a jump ahead, and this book will help every keen gardener to become more professional in being able to recognise weeds in his own garden, and to understand the many different courses of control that are open to him. Take your weeds seriously and gardening as a whole is likely to be more fun. So this is a serious book, yet at the same time an enjoyable one.

The best gardeners use knowledge gained both from their own practical experience and from wider, more theoretic sources. In these pages, many facts are established that would take the average gardener, working on his own, years to discover for himself. Yet the book can be only a beginning, for weeds and soil and other conditions vary sharply, even between adjoining districts. So, take this book out into the garden and perhaps add marginal notes on your own most pervasive weeds and how you have learnt to combat them!

One thing is certain: there is a great deal of misunderstanding about weeds. Elderly gardener-handymen are apt to tell the most ridiculous old wives' tales. Old habits die hard, though the reasons behind them are often lost; new practices are forever regarded with suspicion and indeed their value is frequently thrown away by some careless action. Who has not seen the owner of a new house painstakingly dig over his garden to 'clean it up' in spring, but fail to take follow-up action quickly enough so allowing all the bits of roots of pernicious perennial weeds to start a fresh life? Almost all perennials can be killed by steady 'bleeding' – that is, removing their top growth consistently over months rather than weeks. Conversely, most can be killed by an application of suitable selective weedkiller – and for the best results, the weedkiller should be applied when the growth has reached its full vigour. Of course, many people who start trying to 'bleed' their weeds and panic when they see new growth, change their tactics and apply weedkiller prematurely. Once you have decided on your plan of campaign, keep firmly to it.

Who has not seen a tidy garden become an untidy one too quickly, because the gardener failed to take preventive action soon enough, perhaps lacking time for weed-control through ambitiously undertaking cultivation on too wide a front? Timing can be all important and involves discipline. But it is equally important to gauge how much work you can undertake at peak periods and this book's emphasis on ground-cover plants to smother the soil and prevent weed-growth is therefore sensible. Again, who has not seen a nice weed-free surface that has been carefully mulched or given some other treatment carelessly broken into by a man in heavy boots? Many gardeners fail to recognise the most elementary fact that every ounce of soil is packed with hundreds of seeds which will germinate, given half a chance.

Towards the end of his book, the author turns his attention to the important matter of herbicides. They come in two kinds: those that destroy all green growth by contact but will not touch the seeds, meaning that any unnecessary disturbance of the soil will encourage germination; and those that put a protective germination-preventing film over the soil which obviously ceases to be effective if it is broken into.

A not insignificant part of my own life has been devoted to the struggle against weeds. I have had two spells in commercial horticulture. In the first, like most beginners, I spent much of the time hoe in hand. In the second, just as the new herbicides were being introduced to commercial growers, I introduced practices alien to the Devon countryside. Indeed for the first time since man cultivated the ground, it was possible to do so without disturbing its surface. The raspberry rows remained perfectly weedless year by year. I thus have a personal interest in Mr Boddy's constructive text and take great pleasure in introducing it to an army of gardeners who, I am convinced, will gain much ammunition in the ever-present battle with weeds.

Newton Abbot   David St John Thomas

INTRODUCTION

Whether practised as a profession or a pastime, gardening is not, never was and never will be an easy task, but it is none the less pleasant and rewarding. One has to pit one's energies and skills against the soil, the general climate, the immediate environment and the vagaries of the weather. There are the plants to consider: their needs as to temperature, light, moisture and sustenance, their fads and fancies, their suitability or otherwise for a particular garden or part of a garden, their reaction to the difficulties which man introduces in providing for his own needs which so often have an adverse effect on the good earth and the purity of the atmosphere.

As if all this were not enough, there are other forces of nature to contend with; preying animals and insects, minor forms of plant life which are predatory on the higher plants, and the 'rogues' among these higher plants which are universally known as weeds.

Soil, climate, environment, even the weather, separately or collectively may bring only the occasional problem or disappointment. Animals are seldom an insuperable scourge. Insect pests and fungus and other diseases may damage or even completely ruin our plants and have to be watched for and resisted. But these do not necessarily attack all plants in all places or in all seasons; perhaps the majority have their own particular hosts or can be regarded as localised or occasional marauders.

Not so with weeds. In nature there is an endless fight for survival among plants, and wherever man selects and cultivates to his own design and needs there will be gate-crashers from among the local plant populace which have not been deemed fit to assume a more important role in man's scheme of things. They are not only difficult to keep at bay but usually have such powers of survival and renewal that they attack again and again; so long as man continues to grow his crops or cultivate his garden he will have to contend with the trespassers, the unwanted plants.

That is, perhaps, the most apt description of weeds. They are not necessarily plants of very low caste; they may even be extremely beautiful in their own right and in their natural habitat. Although we may deny them a place within the precincts of a garden, we must nevertheless thank God for them and their ability to clothe the waste places that nature and, in particular, mankind, creates. But in a garden there is no living space for them; we must keep them at bay or ruthlessly extinguish them, and this constitutes the gardener's most constant battle against the forces of nature.

In writing this book I have had the home gardener particularly in mind. He wages a battle year in, year out, against weeds and seldom really gains the upper hand in performing what is, perhaps, the least enjoyable part of gardening – certainly an arduous one. All too often the weeds win and the gardener, once so full of enthusiasm, either has to be satisfied with partial, hard-fought-for results or becomes so discouraged that he gives up the fight. No battle can be won without some knowledge of the tactics of defence and attack. The campaign against weeds can be changed from a frontal attack to calculated defence, resisting the challenge and maintaining the supremacy with far less prolonged effort than is usually expended.

I hope this book will enable the home gardener to sit back more frequently and bask in the pleasant sunshine in a weed-free garden. But do not misunderstand me: there is really no such thing as a permanently weed-free garden. No one has a right to expect to get more out of life than they are prepared to put in, least of all in a garden where one is tending living things; but there is an immeasurable difference between drudgery and enjoying hard toil and its fruits. The passing of knowledge to back up hard work and lighten the load, with the reward that of a garden not only better for the absence of weeds but one made more beautiful and satisfying through the methods adopted to exclude them, was my aim in writing this book.

F. A. B.

PART ONE

INTRODUCING WEEDS

While any unwanted plant can be regarded as a weed, it is always as well to know the enemy, its habits, strength and powers of survival with which is coupled the means of reproduction. Countless plants, both native and introduced, can take on the mantle of weeds and it would need a whole book to cover all the possibilities. Some are widespread, others more localised in that they flourish only in certain soils and conditions. Some present a problem to the arable farmer but seldom cause concern in gardens. Others are normally inhabitants of hedgerows and roadsides or readily populate waste places and may have to be eradicated from a neglected garden or, if thriving close at hand, may transgress into one that is well cultivated.

This part of the book is devoted to grouping and summarising a few of the weeds which are most likely to be encountered in a garden. A brief description of them is given and, equally important, a few words are added about any characteristics which assist weeds to spread or survive and which provide a clue to countermeasures. It should not be assumed, however, that this is any more than a short list of the most important. To cover adequately all those plants which can be termed weeds would, as I have said, occupy a whole volume.

CHAPTER ONE

ANNUAL WEEDS

An annual is a plant which is born from seed, grows, flowers, seeds and dies within one growing season. While perhaps the majority of annuals germinate in spring, some will do so in the autumn and overwinter as seedlings to begin the following season with a head start and able to produce a new crop of seeds in quick time. With no permanent green parts capable of multiplying by vegetative means, true annuals depend for their survival on quick growth and prodigality of seed, not just sufficient to replace the parents but in abundance to counter losses. In harsh, inhospitable and exacting conditions some annuals will come to maturity in double-quick time by flowering and seeding at a very early age, although the plants may be stunted in growth. There is consequently little chance of checking their progress by starving them out.

Seeding, therefore, is the modus operandi to contend with. If we can prevent this we must surely obliterate the species, but here again annual weeds have a counter. The seeds of the majority will lie dormant in the soil for a number of years, germinating only when they are brought near to the surface. Soil cultivations in succeeding years may therefore induce seeds which have been produced years ago and become buried to spring suddenly into life, so it may not be enough to wage a concentrated effort for one year only. Then there are the means by which some are capable of spreading their seeds far and wide. Invasion from the outside is thus always likely, and here the chief invaders will most probably be those plants whose seeds are specially equipped for wind distribution, eg groundsel and sow-thistle. Imported seed-ridden soil, manure or compost may prove a further source of infestation and undoubtedly some seeds may be brought in clinging to the plumage or fur of birds and animals, or via their droppings.

Difficult though perennial weeds with questing roots may be, they do at least reveal themselves and their intentions and are less inclined to become dominant by widespread infiltration from outside. Annual weeds are often a greater menace to the home gardener.

THE UBIQUITOUS ANNUALS

These need little describing for they are universally known. The most widespread of all is annual meadow-grass, *Poa annua*, which has the capacity to spring up anywhere from well-kept lawns and cultivated ground to the harsh, uninviting surface of a gravel path or the merest chink in paving. The minimum of soil and moisture will suffice for germination, and paucity of either, unless there is a prolonged drought, will not be enough to stop the plants from making a modicum of growth and producing seed. Over-wintering plants are the ones to watch for, because with the first signs of spring, reproduction will be on the way to set up the summer flow. Few lawns are without this unwanted grass, many are composed of it largely and, as ornamental grass areas, they are not to be despised. Where this situation prevails one should beware of spreading the weeds via the mowings and the compost heap, for annual meadow-grass will seed even under the closest mowing.

Common chickweed, *Stellaria media*, groundsel (*Senecio vulgaris*) and shepherd's purse (*Capsella bursa-pastoris*) make up a formidable quartet. All will winter as young plants, to begin reproduction in early spring as other seeds of their kind start a more delayed germination. Chickweed sprawls and infiltrates; it is a particular menace to seedling plants from which it cannot be readily disassociated without disturbing them, as it tends to envelop them. Groundsel produces airborne seeds, so it can appear from nowhere. It can be pulled out easily from among seedling plants but it usually comes away with a ball of soil and causes much disturbance. Shepherd's purse may be a little more contained in its habits but it is equally a menace. It comes out cleanly with a

B

Fig 1   1   Hairy bitter-cress, *Cardamine hirsuta*; 2   Red dead-nettle, *Lamium purpureum*; 3   Black bindweed, *Polygonum convolvulus*

taproot when drawn by hand but is so tough at ground level that it is not one of the easiest weeds to hoe out.

INSIDIOUS SEEDERS

Whatever seeding properties the ubiquitous annuals may have, there is no more insidious infiltrator than the hairy bitter-cress, *Cardamine hirsuta*. Another overwinterer with the capacity to spring up in the modicum of soil it will, because of the conditions, flower and seed when in size it seems hardly out of the seedling stage. The time from flowering to seeding is a few days only, and the explosive seed-capsules which burst at the least provocation will fling the seeds out. To stop it seeding, the plant must be dealt with before it starts to flower. Fortunately, although quite common, it is not so universal as those previously described, but where it has settled in it can become an even greater problem.

The red dead-nettle, *Lamium purpureum*, is a widespread weed but it concentrates its attacks to the extent that in some gardens it causes no concern. It is very common on waste ground, where it will form large patches and be quite attractive when covered in early spring with its pinkish-purple flowers. Once it gets a foothold in a garden it can become as great an all-round menace as the other weeds mentioned already.

It is no relation of, nor does it bear any real resemblance to, the true nettles. Of these the annual form, *Urtica urens*, is not so well known as its perennial cousin, the stinging nettle: it tends to be more localised, but it is much more difficult to cope with. Seldom exceeding 25cm (10in) in height, it too starts to seed long before its full stature is reached and can do so even under stunting conditions. It is one of the weeds whose seeds are often imported in manure, or in compost from sewage-works. Germination is usually in the spring.

Several of the speedwells can become real plagues. The really weedy ones have much in common in appearance and in general habit and we need not try to distinguish between the wall speedwell, *Veronica arvensis*, the ivy-leaved speedwell, *V. hederifolia*, the field speedwell, *V. agrestis*, the grey speedwell, *V. polita* or the large or Buxbaum's speedwell, *V. persica*. All are free-seeding annuals with small blue to lilac flowers, often with a whitish lower lip. Except for the wall speedwell which is rather more erect, they are of a procumbent nature, sprawling over the ground in a mat-like manner and becoming entangled with the rightful occupants of the garden much as does the common chickweed. Seeding is profuse from an early age, but with the exception of the wall and ivy-leaved speedwells, overwintering of seedlings is not usual. This latter species prefers the drier soils; the others flourish better in the more fertile garden loams where, once installed, they can become a real problem. They will also establish themselves in a lawn but are not quite such a nuisance in this respect as the perennial creeping speedwell, *V. filiformis*, which will be discussed later in this book.

FROM CORNFIELDS AND WASTE PLACES TO GARDENS

Four of the white 'daisies' so common in cornfields, arable land and on waste ground can become persistent garden weeds locally. They are the mayweed or stinking chamomile, *Anthemis cotula*; the corn chamomile, *A. arvensis*; the scentless mayweed, *Tripleurospermum maritimum* sub-sp. *inodorum* (*Matricaria inodora*); and the wild chamomile, *M. recutita*. All have finely segmented leaves and white daisy-like flowers and can, as a group, be readily recognised. The first of them announces itself for, as its common names imply, it has strongly scented foliage. The foliage of the wild chamomile is pleasantly aromatic rather than strongly pungent; and the white florets of the flower-heads sweep back soon after they open. The corn chamomile occasionally assumes short-lived perennial form. Generally one would not rate these as regular garden invaders, but they may become serious contenders locally.

Spurrey, *Spergula arvensis*, also tends to be localised, preferring acid sandy soils. In the localities where it is abundant it is variously known as devil's-gut, sandweed, yarr and pick-purse. Of thin wiry habit, with small leaves, it has not the appearance of a strong competitor but where it thrives it can be exceedingly prolific. Generally it defers germination until the spring but occasionally there will be some autumn germination and overwintering seedlings.

TWO WEEDY GENERA

The genus *Polygonum* is of Jekyll and Hyde character. It contains perfectly good flowering plants, several of which will be discussed in the section on ground cover, but unfortunately, a number of others which are troublesome weeds. I have selected three of the most common for mention here. The common persicaria, *P. persicaria*, is probably the most widespread although it tends to abound in some localities and be little evident in others. It has a host of common names: redshank, spotted smart-weed, willow-herb, heart-weed, spotted knotweed and lover's-pride. Several of the names give a clue to its identity, for it has reddish stems with swollen nodes and reddish patches on its leaves. The pale persicaria, *P. lapathifolium*, is similar though stronger but, as its name implies, it is not so deeply marked. Both are weeds of fertile soil where they will grow vigorous and lush and soon overwhelm plants. They are often introduced into a garden via imported weed-ridden soil or sewage manure.

Knotgrass or iron-weed, *P. aviculare*, is easily recognised and tends to populate field crops, roadsides and waste places more than gardens. It often comes up in abundance in the spring in the bare places on winter sports fields. Prostrate and sprawling in habit, its flowers are inconspicuous; the toughness of its stems from which its common names derive is its really characteristic feature, making it difficult to hoe out satisfactorily, especially if the surface is panned and hard, a condition it seems to relish more so than most weeds.

Of quite different habit from the majority of its kinfolk, the black bindweed, *P. convolvulus*, is a climbing annual which can become a very real nuisance and one that is difficult to overcome when it starts to scramble over or twine around other plants. Its stems are thin and angular, its leaves small, broadly ovate and acutely pointed, and there should be no difficulty in recognising it. Its flowers are comparatively inconspicuous. It is known by other names such as bearbine, ivy bindweed and cornbine.

Although readily distinguished from them, the fat hen, *Chenopodium album*, has many of the characteristics and habits of the

Fig 2   1 Common persicaria, *Polygonum persicaria*; 2 Spurrey, *Spergula arvensis*; 3 Fumitory, *Fumaria officinalis*

persicarias and can be even more vigorous and enveloping. Its flowers are different – green rather than reddish and in looser racemes – and there is a certain amount of meal on the stems. It too has a number of common names such as pigweed, white goosefoot, bacon-weed, meal-weed and frostblite. Apart from being a real smotherer of plants it is a host for several pests, principally blackfly with which it is often wreathed, especially in a dry summer when aphids of all kinds abound.

PRETTY BUT TROUBLESOME

Except for a long spell in an industrial area where the weeds were principally the ubiquitous ones, I have never had to practise horticulture on one of the really light soils, so I can look upon the common fumitory, *Fumaria officinalis*, as a rather pretty little weed but one which is capable none the less of being quite a pest when it is present in force. Its finely divided glaucous foliage is not un-attractive and it has quite pretty dense racemes of spurred purplish-pink flowers. Where it abounds it is not easy to contain, and it is an overwintering annual which needs attacking early in the spring if it is to be prevented from multiplying rapidly.

Not many weeds can be endearing, but who would not take to those two little violas, the field pansy, *Viola arvensis*, and the heart's-ease, *V. tricolor*? The former has creamy yellow flowers frequently splashed with violet, while *V. tricolor* gets its specific name from its yellow, bluish-violet or pink flowers or combina-tions of these colours. Pretty though they may be, in places where they are abundant they can be frowned upon for, as those who grow garden pansies know full well, regeneration by self-sown seedlings is a pronounced feature.

SOW-THISTLES AND OTHERS

Milk or sow-thistles are widely distributed and well known. They are very much like true thistles in general appearance although crisper and more succulent plants with glossy, slightly glaucous leaves. They exude a milky juice when severed. Although annuals, they have deeply penetrating taproots which are difficult to draw out by hand unless the soil is fairly deep and loose for, when grasped, the plants readily break off at ground level and the rootstocks remaining will soon grow again. Like many members of the daisy family they have airborne seeds, and so can drift in from outside and soon spread around. They do tend to appear more as individuals rather than in dense colonies: this is fortunate, since given the opportunity they soon make massive plants. They overwinter as young seedlings and make rapid growth in the spring. Normal methods of annual weed-control will exterminate them. Isolated plants in difficult places can be readily killed by spot treatment of the flat basal rosettes of leaves with a little selective weedkiller. The main difference between the common milk or sow-thistle, *Sonchus oleraceus*, and the spiny milk or sow-thistle, *S. asper*, is denoted by their common names.

Several of the spurges are weeds of arable land and gardens, the most widely distributed being the petty spurge, *Euphorbia peplus*, which is an annual herb growing 15–25cm (6–10in) high with spirally arranged leaves and inconspicuous flowers enclosed by yellowish-green bracts. The whole plant exudes a milky juice. This is another of those annual weeds which in places can be quite prolific and come high on the black list.

The marsh cudweed, *Gnaphalium uliginosum*, can be placed in much the same category as liable to be very troublesome locally. It prefers light but damp soils where it forms a dwarf, rather spreading plant with woolly stems and leaves giving an overall greyish appearance. The plant as a whole, and in particular the brownish-yellow flower-heads, remind me of the rather revered edelweiss, a personal and perhaps not very apt impression but one which affords a clue to recognition.

Those to whom geraniums mean only the zonal pelargoniums so popular for bedding, will hardly expect a true geranium to be regarded as a weed. The dove's-foot cranesbill, *Geranium molle*, is not without some modest beauty: it has small, single, rosy-purple flowers over deeply notched rounded leaves with reddish stalks produced from a rosette-like plant. Quite common, although it does prefer the lighter soils, it is a weed of the lawn as well as other parts of the garden, its rosettes becoming flattened and stunted but surviving below the blades of the mowing-machine.

Generally it germinates in the autumn, so it is one of those early-spring starters.

Finally there is a garden escape which has become a weed in many places. The opium poppy, *Papaver somniferum*, with its smooth glaucous leaves and large double white or pale lilac flowers, is familiar to many. In some gardens it is tolerated, not without some justification, for it is quite ornamental; but like most poppies it is very prolific of seed and once well established may take several years to eradicate.

CHAPTER TWO

SEEDING PERENNIAL WEEDS

A perennial is a plant which lives for an indefinite number of years, growing taller or wider, or both, with each successive year. It may be of a woody nature such as trees, shrubs and most climbing plants; or a herb which either retains its growth and is probably evergreen, or dies down to the ground each year and renews its growth annually, in which case it is termed herbaceous.

Perennials may not depend wholly on their sexual capacity resulting in seed production for the perpetuation and spread of the species. Many of them are better equipped to increase more surely by vegetative means and these we shall be looking at in the next two chapters. Here I have tried to segregate a few which can be rated prolific seed-producers and, as weeds, have to be reckoned with more by this capacity than by their vegetative spread.

CHIEFLY LAWN WEEDS

The common daisy, *Bellis perennis*, and the dandelion, *Taraxacum officinale*, need no introduction. The plantains, of which there are three species generally to be contended with, are well known also. The great or broad-leaved plantain, *Plantago major*, is the most widespread, varying from the lush growth attained on roadsides and waste ground to the flattened rosettes of leaves formed under the restricted conditions of a lawn, rosettes which may spread individually and kill all grass within a diameter of about 10cm (4in). The ribwort plantain, *P. lanceolata*, which is as widespread but usually rather less prolific on lawns, can do just as much damage with its rosettes of much narrower leaves. The hoary plantain, *P. media*, is more localised; it is less vigorous than the other two species but it too forms dense, flattened rosettes of ovate leaves with the same suffocating powers.

In similar vein the cat's-ear, *Hypochaeris radicata*, is a not infrequent invader of lawns. Under such conditions this also develops a close rosette of lanceolate, toothed and hairy basal leaves from which in late summer, given the chance, it will thrust up long flowering stems bearing small dandelion-like flowers.

These are among the commonest of lawn weeds but, by nature of the broad flattened front they present, they are the easiest to control by modern herbicidal treatment. A more insidious weed and one which is just as widespread and just as much of a nuisance in other parts of the garden, especially in the rock garden, is the procumbent pearlwort, *Sagina procumbens*, which is often mistaken for a moss. It has no affinity to this, being a flowering plant which of all things belongs to the same family as the carnation and the pink, but it certainly has a moss-like habit with its thin wiry stems set with small narrow leaves, composing a close flat mat. Its tiny white flowers are produced above and among this flat growth and the majority of them will escape the blades of the mower, so on the lawn there is little reduction of seeding. The seeds will lie dormant beneath and protected by the top mat of growth which, if removed, enables the seeds to germinate and one is then back where one started. Although resistant to some of the selective weedkillers, it will succumb to others, as we shall see later. Elsewhere it may be somewhat easier to eliminate but, starting to seed while very young and being capable of growing in the modicum of soil, early and constant attacks upon it are necessary if one is to gain the upper hand.

Another member of the same family, the mouse-ear chickweed, *Cerastium holosteoides* (*C. vulgatum*, *C. triviale*), can be a serious invader of a lawn, being a widespread weed on most soils, although it does really prefer those of a chalky or sandy nature. Its slender stems creep over the ground and form dense mats in much the same way as does the common chickweed, from which it can be distinguished by its hairy leaves which, no doubt, have something to do with its resistance to some forms of selective weedkiller.

WIND-BORNE MENACES

Plants whose seeds can be dispersed by the wind for either short or long distances are sure to produce progeny in places where they will be unwelcome and many of the most prolific seed-bearers among perennial weeds have this characteristic. The dandelion must again come into the reckoning for it is a common weed in places other than lawns and grassland. Millions of stock plants in pasture-land, on roadsides and on waste ground ensure that no garden can be counted free of the plague.

Of the numerous forms of thistle the creeping thistle, *Cirsium arvense*, is by far the most common. It is responsible for most of the thistle-down which is dispersed for considerable distances in late summer, causing many home gardeners much concern. Strangely, however, this is less of a menace than is generally supposed, for it consists mostly of the plumed parachute-like attachments which have parted from the seed, leaving it in the seed-head.

Around the same time the plumed seeds of the willow-herbs also come floating through the air. The two commonest species are the great hairy willow-herb, *Epilobium hirsutum*, known also as codlins and cream, which grows on the banks of streams and lakes and in marshy places; and the rose-bay willow-herb, *Chamaenerion (Epilobium) angustifolium*, which so often takes over places laid waste by man or nature, inhabits woodlands and clearings and furnishes these with masses of rosy-purple flowers on tall stems. I would not rate either of these garden weeds of the highest importance unless they are growing naturally in quantity in close proximity; but there is a lesser member of the tribe which I have found to be a much greater nuisance. It is the small-flowered, hairy willow-herb, *Epilobium parviflora*, which is much smaller in all its parts than the two previously mentioned, its flowering stems reaching a height of 20–60cm (8–24in) according to its growing conditions. Its small rosy flowers do not unfold in quantity at any one time but are quickly productive of long seed-pods and airborne seeds whether the plants are lush of growth or stunted by the paucity of their foothold.

Fig 3   1   Ribwort plantain, *Plantago lanceolata*; 2   Mouse-ear
chickweed, *Cerastium holosteoides*; 3   Procumbent pearlwort, *Sagina
procumbens*; 4   Cat's-ear, *Hypochaeris radicata*

The docks may not have quite the same powers of seed distribution but, although they lack the plumes of the dandelion and the willow-herbs, their seeds, being flat and light, do get blown around. There are two main species: the broad-leaved dock, *Rumex obtusifolius*, and the curled dock, *R. crispus*. They need no further description. Apart from their undesirability in any place in the garden, they are also hosts for blackfly with which their flowering stems become festooned in seasons when the fly is widespread. This in itself is sufficient reason to put them on the black list.

The coltsfoot, *Tussilago farfara*, another plant of roadsides and waste ground, has more often to be contended with when one is taking over a neglected garden or constructing one on land which was left to run wild before being built on. None the less, as it has the plumed seeds typical of so many of the daisy family, if it is abundant in the vicinity there is always a chance of an invasion. This plant produces its small dandelion-like flowers very early in the spring before its broad grey-green leaves appear, and the absence of leaves tends to make one forget that weeds are on the move and so overlook the necessity for destroying the flowers before they seed.

TREES IN THE WIND

We do not normally regard trees as weeds, but some can certainly take on this role. One needs only to have the common ash and sycamore growing in close proximity to be brought face to face with the fact that their seedlings, germinating in all manner of places, can quickly lose their charm of being baby trees. In a normal breeze the winged seeds will flutter over great areas, and in an autumn gale they can travel appreciable distances. Springing up between plants they can be dispatched readily with a touch of the hoe, but they have a habit of lodging in the crowns of herbaceous plants, thrusting up in a hedge or becoming entangled with the rootstock of a shrub. Pulling them out from these positions is no easy matter, for by the time their stems have become woody, their taproots have gained a fair hold of the ground. If they cannot be drawn out they are best cut off and the ends of the stumps treated with a brushwood killer.

The willows may not be such widespread invaders, but where the common goat sallow, or pussy-willow *Salix caprea*, abounds, a similar problem may present itself. I know, for I am forever pulling out the wretched seedlings! If trees are in the locality there is not much one can do about their fluffy windborne seeds. They are not really trees for the home garden but many people, because of their love of the delightful late-winter catkins, like to have a tree just around the corner. They should make sure that they have the non-seeding male form with golden catkins and not the inferior silver of the female.

I am also plagued with seedling silver birches, for I have a number of mature trees in my garden. Everybody's favourite, these trees are being planted in increasing numbers everywhere and I often wonder whether those who plant them in quite small gardens fully appreciate what they are letting themselves in for. In the first place, a mature silver birch is usually far too big for the average home garden and while it will not cast dense shade it does produce masses of fibrous roots just below the surface. These quickly gobble up moisture, natural or applied, and make it exceedingly difficult to establish plants beneath. While they are still only striplings they will be on the production cycle. Annually I sweep up their small flat seeds by the bucketful from my terrace, seeds which are light and which get wafted around to germinate in hordes, even in the cracks between paving. They can therefore sometimes take on the characteristics of weeds.

NON-FLOWERING PLANTS

The difference between the seed of a flowering plant and the spore of a non-flowering one may be appreciable, but their purpose is the same: that of sexual reproduction. Fungi of all sorts have to be reckoned with in a garden, principally those which are responsible for plant diseases; but these generally are outside the title of weeds. Mosses need no description and we shall be discussing them in more detail later. Lichens and algae on plants, on the soil surface and in water come more within the category of maladies; but liverworts are indeed weeds. Generally I would say that they are of more concern to the producer of plants than to the home gardener, especially anyone concerned with the raising of plants in containers. They are readily recognised by their flat, green, leaf-like structures from which arise the spore-bearing stems. These should be skimmed off together with the top soil, if they are to be prevented from multiplying rapidly, which they are liable to do under moist-soil conditions.

CHAPTER THREE

PERENNIAL WEEDS WITH PENETRATING ROOTS

Spread and reproduction by vegetative means is more insidious and difficult to contend with when it takes place below ground. Many gardeners consider weeds with this habit the worst ones to cope with. I believe that the weeds which are most likely to be forever with us are the annuals, with their greater sexual productivity; but I do concede that, among the perennials, those which become firmly entrenched and go wandering below ground are by far the most perverse.

There are roughly two classes: those with deep anchoring roots and those with meandering roots or underground stems which extend far and wide and have the capacity to produce shoots and form colonies. Here I will offend the purists by choosing to regard all underground portions of a plant as roots, although in fact the majority do their colonising by means of underground stems called either rhizomes or stolons. Whatever the method the end product is the same.

DOCKS, DANDELIONS AND NETTLES

No more really needs to be said about the first two. They have no vegetative means of reproduction or spread other than by growing larger and more prolific of seed if they are left to thrive. Their deep anchoring roots concern us here; the answer to which will be found in Part Four.

The common stinging nettle, *Urtica dioica*, often comes into the reckoning when one is creating a garden from the wild or taking over a neglected one, or when the weed is able to infiltrate from adjoining land. In the preparation of the ground the nettle is not difficult to clear out, for its underground stems are tough and if the ground is reasonably loose it can be dug or even pulled out lock, stock and barrel. And there are easier ways than man-handling, to get rid of this nuisance at the outset.

The white dead-nettle or white archangel, *Lamium album*, is not a relative although it has some foliage affinity. It too is primarily a force to be reckoned with when one is constructing a garden rather than an invader of one under cultivation and, like the stinging nettle, it is not too difficult to tackle when the battle-ground is open.

SOME REALLY DIFFICULT ONES

The couch-grass, *Agropyron repens*, is noted for being a tenacious transgressor. Every gardener will be familiar with it as couch, scutch, twitch or wickens and will know full well how it spreads by underground stolons and how every little bit left in the ground can grow again to produce another plant. It is not alone among grasses for others have its spreading tendency, if to a lesser degree. The chief of them is the creeping soft-grass, *Holcus mollis*. This often becomes established and forms large patches in lawns which are laid with low-quality turf or are not well cared for.

Another bane of the home gardener's life is ground elder, *Aegopodium podagraria*, known also as bishop's weed, goutweed or goatweed and herb Gerard. This is an offensive plant with its persistent spread, its rank smell when handled and its obdurate nature. Generally it seems to filter into a garden from surrounding hedgerows, waste land or neglected adjacent gardens. It likes to lurk at the base of a hedge or around the rootstocks of spreading shrubs, doing no particular damage there but forever trying to break out. It is a really difficult one to counter, for not only are its underground stems akin to those of couch in their questing and establishing powers and in their opposition to extraction, but it is also very resistant to herbicides other than those which can be safely applied only to ground which is not cropped.

The common horse-tail, *Equisetum arvense*, is a non-flowering plant capable of taking a grip on any soil, from the driest and

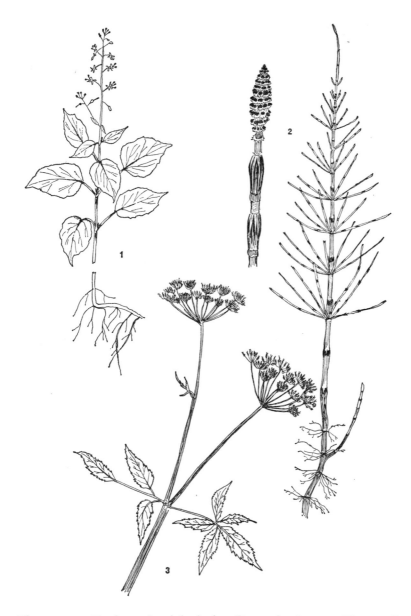

Fig 4   1 Enchanter's nightshade, *Circaea lutetiana*; 2 Horse-tail,
Equisetum arvense, showing fertile and sterile stems; 3   Ground elder,
Aegopodium podagraria

most inhospitable to that which is extremely wet; and what a hold
it takes. It is sometimes said that one can be plagued with it in life
and after death and I can support this half-truth for I have seen
its long, wiry, dark brown rhizomes brought up from several feet
below the surface in the excavation of graves. There seems little
hope therefore of weedkillers being wholly effective: certainly
not the contact ones or those taken in through the roots. Even the
foliage translocated ones have long distances to travel to kill out-
right, for removal of every bit of stem and root down to the normal depths of cultivation is no guarantee that the plant will not
thrust up its shoots again from remains below this depth. If it is
persistently denied the chance to flourish above ground it can
eventually be weakened out of existence. It is known locally as
meadow-pine, pine-grass, fox-tail rush, scouring rush, bottle
brush, horse-pipes and snake-grass. The fertile shoots appear
above ground in the spring, the sterile ones later and the spores
are dispersed by wind and other means.

Bracken, *Pteridium aquilinum*, exhibits similar characteristics
below ground, for its thick fleshy rhizomes extend very deeply
and have the same recuperative powers. This is an inhabitant of
woodland and moorland. It normally comes within a gardener's
sphere only when he takes over such land for cultivation and he
usually has to rid himself of it by persistent retaliation.

MORE SUBTERRANEAN CREEPERS

The stout scaly stolons of coltsfoot do not penetrate deeply. They
are quite easy to fork out and the foliage is receptive to translocated herbicides if this weed has to be faced when a garden is
being made. A really determined attack at the onset should
eliminate it and chance seedlings afterwards will not be too difficult to destroy. The creeping thistle is rather more tenacious and
must be tackled with persistency, possibly over an indefinite
period.

Those whose gardens have been converted from woodland are
more likely to have to face the challenge of the lesser celandine,
Ranunculus ficaria, the dog's mercury, *Mercurialis perennis*, and the
enchanter's nightshade, *Circaea lutetiana*. I can vouch for the prob-

lems these present, for my own garden was hewn out of woodland surroundings.

The lesser celandine is the most widespread of the trio, for in nature it also grows in meadows and on the banks of streams, so it is the one most likely to be encountered. It has an underground system of club-shaped tubers which readily break off when the plant is disturbed and give rise to new plants. Burying the remains deeply is no answer, for shoots will emerge from the tubers at a spade's depth or more below the surface. I have 'killed off' the plants with selective weedkillers only to find them emerging as strongly as ever the following year. Whatever remedy is applied it must be persevered with.

This too can be said of enchanter's nightshade, a plant with white, creeping, underground stems which are very brittle and exceedingly difficult to extract, especially if the soil is moist and heavy: it revels in this. It wends its way into and through plants, but if as many as possible of the underground stems are removed when the ground is being prepared, and any surviving plants are repeatedly checked by hand, hoe or chemical, it will eventually fade out. Like all weeds of this kind, however, given a few weeks' respite and the chance to make some top growth, it will soon start to re-establish itself.

The dog's mercury is one of the few plants which will carpet the ground beneath beech trees and as such will be known to many, if not by name. Like the beeches it is happiest on calcareous soils. Away from the shade of the woodland it is less at home, so it is not really a common weed of gardens. Where it has been established before man took over, it may take some time to be eradicated for, like the enchanter's nightshade, it has long creeping rhizomes.

WANDERERS ABOVE AND BELOW GROUND

As was said earlier of the annual black bindweed, *Polygonum convolvulus*, climbing weeds are a particular nuisance. There are two perennials which are even worse than this annual: the larger bindweed or bell-bine, *Calystegia sepium*, which was formerly *Convolvulus* and is often known simply by this name; and the dwarf or field bindweed or, again, bell-bine, *Convolvulus arvensis*.

Fig 5   1 Couch-grass, *Agropyron repens*; 2 Lesser celandine,
Ranunculus ficaria; 3 Dwarf bindweed, *Convolvulus arvensis*

Of the two, while the latter may wander around a garden and use herbaceous and other plants for support, it is by no means as all-enveloping in its habits as is the larger bindweed. This in nature can be quite a picturesque sight when it twines itself over bushes and hedgerows, fences, or low-growing scrub and festoons them with large, funnel-shaped, white flowers. It spreads by means of white rhizomes: these are not very deeply placed in the ground but they are brittle and extremely difficult to winkle out from among the roots of a hedge or a bush. Left alone, while it may to some extent charm with its floral display, its lush growth will eventually cause the deterioration of any branches which it envelops.

The dwarf bindweed, with small white or pink flowers, is a rather insidious little nuisance. It will climb to a height of 75 cm (30in) or more, but being thin of stem and small in leaf it probably has more of a retarding effect on small plants than on bushes, and when it gets mixed up with them and other weeds a tangled mass has to be sorted out. Above ground, herbicides are difficult to apply; but by forking out the roots, chopping off every little bit of growth as soon as it appears above the surface and, if necessary, resorting to dipping the points of climbing shoots in selective weedkiller as previously described, it is possible to gain the upper hand of these two closely allied weeds.

CHAPTER FOUR

MAT-FORMING PERENNIAL WEEDS

These weeds also spread and colonise but more openly than those
described in the previous chapter, for they do it above ground
by means of runners, stolons or prostrate stems which root as
they grow and form new plants. They are generally less difficult
to control than the underground creepers, but they can present an
almost equal problem when they penetrate into the crowns of
plants or find their way into a lawn and take root.

LAWN INVADERS

The commonest of all is the wild white clover, *Trifolium repens*. In
the right place, this plant has many virtues: it is an important
component of pasture-land and is invaluable for adding to grass-
seed mixtures for roadside banks and places where soil erosion is
a problem, for its prostrate stems root at the joints and stabilise
the soil surface. This propensity switches to the liability side when
the plant gets into turf mown for recreational purposes, for when
subject to lots of wear it quickly becomes slippery. Although its
presence in an ornamental lawn may have less significance, it is
usually frowned upon. It will start as quite small plants and infiltrate between the grasses. While these are growing vigorously it
does not make its presence felt either in action or appearance;
but during a prolonged drought, when the grass loses its vigour
and turns brown unless watered, the patches of clover will remain
green and thriving, will increase with the lack of competition
from the grass and will merge into still larger patches which in
time will dominate the lawn.

A close cousin, the lesser yellow trefoil, *T. dubium*, has more

Fig 6   1   Creeping buttercup, *Ranunculus repens*; 2   Lesser yellow
trefoil, *Trifolium dubium*; 3   Creeping speedwell, *Veronica filiformis*

slender, wiry stems, smaller leaves and small knobs of yellow flowers. Although it appears to be less vigorous it can be an equal nuisance and just as resistant, if not more so, to selective weed-killers. There is one advantage: the prostrate stems of the young plants do not start to root at the nodes quite so early in life as do those of the wild white clover, and they can be pulled out quite easily in their entirety by teasing up the stems with an old knife in order to get a good grip of the crown, then thrusting in the knife, prising up and drawing out the whole plant, including the tap-root. Thus the removal of one small plant will prevent the formation of a colony which would demand more extensive treatment.

The finely divided feathery foliage of yarrow or milfoil, *Achillea millefolium*, is not looked upon with favour in a lawn, for it can eventually dominate large patches of turf which during drought will be prominent as green areas. In nature the yarrow is a much taller, less prostrate grower, producing upright stems bearing flat heads of white flowers which become tinged with pink as they age. These flowers, when cut and dried, make quite attractive decorating material for indoors.

The bugle, *Ajuga reptans*, and the self-heal, *Prunella vulgaris*, are closely allied and have much similarity when they are kept stunted by the mowing-machine. Both in nature are very presentable wild flowers and both have garden forms which make very useful ground cover: I shall be discussing these later. The blue flowers of the bugle, rising from the cone-shaped inflorescences, are better known than the pinkish-violet ones of the self-heal. Of the two the latter is probably the more troublesome as a lawn weed, for it can spread into quite dominating patches and is inclined to be resistant to some of the selective lawn herbicides.

So too is the creeping speedwell, *Veronica filiformis*. In a lawn this will augment its annual cousins which drift in and, being a perennial and less dependent for survival on seeding – close mowing does restrict this activity – it can be more difficult to exterminate. It can be readily distinguished from the annual forms by its thinner prostrate stems and smaller leaves. It has blue to lilac flowers, produced singly, and a patch growing naturally can be a quite pretty sight. The thyme-leaved speedwell, *V. serpylli-folia*, has even smaller leaves, more oval in shape and with almost entire margins. Its flowers, too, are smaller and are white, veined blue. Both forms root freely from the joints and in the moist soils they appreciate they can soon form large colonies.

By its leaves the field wood rush, *Luzula campestris*, known locally as Good Friday grass and sweep's brush, can be mistaken at first for a very coarse-leaved grass, but it is soon recognised when its spherical clusters of brown, typically rush-like flowers are thrust up on short stems in the spring. It spreads by means of short creeping stolons and, once firmly entrenched, the patches will gradually extend and become quite distinctive among the grasses. For reasons which will be mentioned later, selective herbicides have little effect, and it may be necessary to resort to manual means of eradicating the plant. Thus, where it does tend to be prevalent – despite being a rush it is by no means averse to the drier soils – action should be taken as soon as it puts in an appearance.

MORE GENERAL SPREADERS

No place is safe from trespass by the creeping buttercup, *Ranunculus repens*. Buttercups in mown lawns are invariably of this species, not their more upright cousins which make old pastures a carpet of gold in the spring, for these do not flourish under close-mown conditions and are not serious weeds of cultivated ground except, perhaps, when they abound in fields alongside gardens. The creeping form wends its way everywhere by means of its strawberry-like runners which root and produce plants at every joint. In loose soil one can pull these up in lengths but where the soil is more solid or sticky each plantlet will have to be dug out by hand or hoe, or some chemical means of eradication adopted. There are also seeds to be contended with, and flowering continues on and off throughout the summer.

Of similar habit and liable to grow in both lawn and cultivated parts of the garden, the creeping cinquefoil, *Potentilla reptans*, and the silverweed, *P. anserina*, are quite common. Both have yellow strawberry-like flowers. The latter, as its common name implies, can be readily distinguished by its silvery, long, finely divided leaves; it is perhaps more an inhabitant of the roadside than a

Fig 7   1   Creeping yellow cress, *Rorippa sylvestris*; 2   Field wood-
rush, *Luzula campestris*; 3   Sheep's sorrel, *Rumex acetosella*

troublesome garden weed. The cinque-foil is of less dense habit. It has palmate leaves and can at times be almost as great a nuisance as the creeping buttercup.

Common everywhere except on the chalky soils, the sheep's sorrel, *Rumex acetosella*, flourishes in particular where the conditions are fairly dry and poor. It has a host of local names such as horse sorrel, cow sorrel, mountain sorrel, red-top sorrel, sour-weed, sower-grass and red-weed. The leaves are hastate, ie arrow-shaped with two side protrusions at the base, and the plant produces erect flower stems with the typical, reddish flowers of the docks to which it is closely allied. It spreads by means of long thin rhizomes, just below the surface, which give rise to new plants. A single seedling, if left unchecked, can in one season extend its influence over a quite large area.

Although I have never come up against it in gardens – but I have no doubt others have – the sight of the creeping yellow cress, *Rorippa sylvestris*, makes me apprehensive, for I have had much contact with it in a broader field and have seen it firmly established and defiant in nurseries. Closely allied to the water-cress it has much more finely divided leaves, yellow flowers and rapidly spreads by stolons into dense, enveloping colonies. I have found it most resistant to herbicides, even to paraquat which normally quickly destroys all top growth, and I have had to resort to much more drastic measures to rid the ground of a weed which, once firmly entrenched, can literally take over. Fortunately, it appears to be localised rather than ubiquitous; but I would counsel those who visit nurseries, see it in existence and purchase stock to be very careful that they do not introduce it into their gardens.

CHAPTER FIVE

INVASIVE GARDEN PLANTS

Although in the Introduction to this book I described a weed as an unwanted plant, I must emphasise that not every plant for which there is no place in a garden is necessarily a weed. It all depends on the plants' willingness to confine themselves to the territory allotted to them or to leave it when required to do so and not return. Often we introduce plants and then regret it, for they will persist in attempting to interfere with others or they have such powers of regeneration that they spring up in all sorts of places and tend to assume the mantle of weeds. A lot depends on the character and size of a garden: in one a particular plant will be an asset, in another a disruptive factor. It is natural that many of our garden plants should exhibit some tenacity and powers of reproduction and survival, and need curbing from time to time. It is only when they are really territorially ambitious that they are apt to become a nuisance. One might say, 'Why plant them at all?' The answer is that not everyone knows their vices and they are often freely offered by the nurseryman who seldom draws attention to these vices.

GROUND COVER UNLIMITED

Although there is more detailed mention of their usefulness in certain situations when we come to the section on planting for ground cover, a preliminary warning must be given about the need to be most careful not to introduce the winter heliotrope, *Petasites fragrans*, or the dwarf bamboo, *Arundinaria vagans*, into a garden without first giving careful consideration to their strong invasive tendencies; or to plant the popular snow-in-summer,

Cerastium tomentosum, in association with choicer plants in a rock-garden without taking due account of its habit of forming an ever-spreading, rooted carpet. Neither should one overlook similar qualities in some of the other very good ground coverers which will be featured as garden assets in Part Three of this book.

MORE SPREADERS

Many of our garden plants spread out and consume space. We can with advantage use some of these for ground cover, but others are not suitable for such a role and need to be in a different setting, for they can become a nuisance to others. This is so with the dotted loosestrife, *Lysimachia punctata,* whose whorls of yellow flowers on 90cm (36in) stems in July and August will grace the pool side or wilder places where there is either strong competition or room to spread without undue restriction; but it can become a positive nuisance in an herbaceous border. In the herbaceous border also, I have found the popular and extremely useful cut-flower, the sneezewort, *Achillaea ptarmica* and its cultivars, very apt to spread and thrust into other plants.

One has to be circumspect in planting those two charming silver-foliaged plants, the white sage, *Artemisia ludoviciana,* and the dwarfer *A. baumgartenii* (*A. villarsii*) with more finely divided leaves. Both have a capacity for rapid sideways expansion, often thrusting out their underground stems well beyond their normal spread and producing plants outside the general clump. One has also to be most careful in siting the soapwort, *Saponaria officinalis* and its cultivars with double flowers. I know of one garden, neglected by its previous owner, where the double pink form has spread everywhere by means of its creeping rootstock and has become most difficult to eradicate.

The oxalis are delightful little plants, but several are such inveterate spreaders that they can quickly become a menace. The pretty little wood sorrel, *Oxalis acetosella* regarded by some as the 'shamrock', and its forms are among the worst for transgressing, with their creeping scaly roots. So too are *O. corniculata* and *O. rubra* (*O. floribunda* of gardens) whose bulbous rhizomes can soon become distributed and develop into large patches.

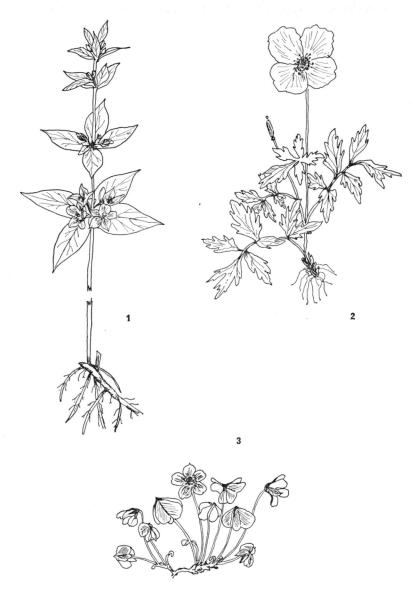

Fig 8   1 Dotted loosestrife, *Lysimachia punctata*; 2 Welsh poppy,
Meconopsis cambrica; 3 Wood sorrel, *Oxalis acetosella*

When I first occupied my present house a rocky bank was studded with the cypress spurge, *Euphorbia cyparissias* and the English stonecrop, *Sedum anglicum*. The former produces 30–45cm (12–18in) high annual stems densely set all round with narrow, light green leaves which give it the rather attractive appearance of a flue-brush. These stems are surmounted by the typical, yellow-green bracts of the spurges and the foliage turns to clear yellow in the autumn. It is a quite pretty plant and useful for ground cover in the right place, but it spreads far and wide by underground shoots and can become a nuisance. By continuous effort I have cleared the bank, having first transferred a few plants to a rather stony wild corner, in full sun, where their activities are naturally restricted.

Sedum anglicum has white flowers tinged with pink and is not seen so often in gardens as is the yellow-flowered biting stonecrop, *S. acre*. The latter in particular would be a most useful garden plant with its sheets of flowers but both species, in addition to spreading sideways to form wide mats, can become plagues, for every little bit of brittle stem which is broken off is liable to take root somewhere. Yet one sees both offered for sale at prices equal to those of rock-garden plants of much higher caste.

All gardeners know how quickly and how far the common garden mint, *Mentha spicata*, can spread. So too can the more ornamental species like the apple mint, *M. rotundifolia*, the pineapple mint, *M. piperita*, and others which, for their aromatic foliage, one might be tempted to plant round a garden pool.

These few examples are just pointers to the need to treat with circumspection any plant which quickly spreads and readily multiplies by vegetative means, not condemning it out of hand but considering first whether there is a place in the garden where its worst characteristics can be turned to assets.

SEEDING MENACES

Some garden plants are so prolific of seed that they can become almost as troublesome as annual weeds. As my garden is situated in a woodland clearing, I am forever seeking to establish dominance over seedlings of the common foxglove. Even those who

D

grow the garden strains can have the same problem and need to remove the spikes of flower-pods before the ones farthest down start to ripen, even if the apex is still bearing the last of the flowers. The Welsh poppy, *Meconopsis cambrica*, is a quite endearing little plant, with its finely cut leaves and yellow flowers. I find strays here and there in my woodland but it never multiplies to any extent. Plant it in a shady rock-garden, however, and allow it to seed and a colony will soon result which, if not kept strictly in check, may eventually become something of a nuisance.

Forget-me-nots too are always with me; I never have to grow any specially for the limited amount of spring bedding which I do. Few would be without them at that season, but there is little one can do to prevent the seeding which takes place before the floral display is over. One can only be careful not to spread the seeds when removing the plants to make way for those which are to succeed them for the summer.

That much loved old garden plant, *Lunaria biennis*, known as honesty, is just as much appreciated for its flat white seed-capsules as for its lilac, purple or white flowers. It contrives to spring up here, there and everywhere from self-sown seedlings. The orange-red seed-pods of the Chinese lantern plant, *Physalis franchetii*, are ideal for drying and for using for winter decoration as a contrast to those of honesty. This is another plant with the ability to reproduce itself. So too does the pot marigold, *Calendula*, which, once grown for its continuous summer flowering, can reappear in strength in ensuing years from the plenteous crop of seed that is cast.

Lastly, mention must be made of yet another plant which is typical of the old cottage form of gardening, *Corydalis lutea*. When present it is more often than not in abundance, springing up from self-sown seed in all manner of places, often furnishing stone walls with its finely-divided foliage and continuous succession of yellow flowers throughout the summer.

*   *   *

I have done no more than mention just a few of the quite common garden plants which have the capacity to outgrow their welcome;

a reminder that 'weed' can be a rather far-reaching term, one which is not necessarily confined to the less pleasing members of the plant kingdom who seek to extend their influence beyond the bounds of the countryside and those places where nature and man decree that they shall be allowed to flourish.

PART TWO

DEFENCE AGAINST WEEDS

No good general relies solely on offensive measures to protect his
territory. He must expect to be attacked and counter-attacked and
must, therefore, also have an eye to defence. The building and
manning of defences are best done before the enemy strikes or, if
it has been necessary to oust him first, before a counter-attack is
launched.

So it is with the gardener in his fight against weeds. He will be
more likely to come out on top with the least effort and losses if
from the start he abandons complacency and prepares for the
fight which is sure to follow. The way he constructs his garden,
the way he plants it and, perhaps above all, how he links these
with his ability to cope with problems in the future, will be the
deciding factor in whether looking after the garden and the
results obtained are to be a pleasure or a burden.

Much of this is anticipation and common sense, but so often
these attributes tend to become overwhelmed by enthusiasm. This
part of the book is intended to help those creating gardens and
others contemplating alterations in layout, to plan and plant as
part of the campaign against the inevitable menace of weeds.

CHAPTER SIX

BUILDING THE DEFENCES

The first essentials of good planning are vision and forethought, not only as to what the finished product will look like and what visual satisfaction it will give but also as to what time and money will be needed to maintain the garden in the best possible condition. In planning a garden and putting the plans into effect everyone must be guided by financial considerations, but it should never be forgotten that the initial cost in time and money has to be borne once only, whereas aftercare goes on indefinitely. It is foolish to plan, construct and plant in such a way that one is quite unable to keep pace with requirements in after years, or to skimp construction and have to contend with the outcome. Not the least problem of aftercare will be an unending fight against weeds: in writing this book I have been conscious that I can do no more than offer suggestions to lighten the burden of that battle. How often are weeds taken into account when one is formulating schemes for layout and putting them into effect?

Without the basis of a theme to work on, it is difficult to say, 'Don't do this or that when planning a garden or you will be creating a weed problem.' Perhaps this looking ahead and preparing defences against the common enemy of the gardener is more a question of constructional details which I shall discuss presently. At least, with one eye on the weed problem, we can plan so that there are the fewest possible 'pockets' where weeds can readily establish themselves and prove difficult to attack, and one can also plan to make counter-measures by manual, chemical and other means as uncomplicated as possible.

Beds and borders should be of simple outline, not necessarily formal, for flowing lines are just as easy to negotiate with a mower if they are not made too squiggly – which in any case is bad design. The same principle should be followed for paths: these should be either straight or with sensible curves inserted with a purpose, ie to go round an object, and not just for the sake of getting away from a straight line. That object – a bed, a tree or shrub – can be inserted if it is not already in existence. Sharp bends and corners should be avoided if possible, for they so often create little 'pockets' which are difficult to clothe or keep clean.

Never build a rock-garden or other feature which will require a lot of attention, especially weeding, if there is a severe limit on the time which can be devoted to looking after the garden. Better by far to have a simple but tasteful layout which can be kept in good order than one which will spell frustration and disappointment later.

CLEANING THE GROUND

This can be the key to the weed problem when constructing a garden or when preparing ground for plants of all types, either short-term or long-term subjects, but particularly the latter. It is especially important in the fight against perennial weeds with deep penetrating roots, or creeping, self-propagating roots and stems. As much as possible of such weed growth should be dug out and burnt. Every little bit left behind will be liable to grow again and produce another plant, especially in the case of such virulent and persistent invaders as couch-grass, ground elder, horse-tail and bindweed whose roots or underground stems readily break up in the course of removal.

Fallowing the ground, ie leaving it bare for a time after its initial cultivation and before planting any subjects which will occupy it without disturbance for a number of years, will enable further attacks to be made on any survivors. This is also an excellent method of reducing the population of those weeds which rely mainly or wholly on reproduction from seeds. There is an old saying, 'One year's seeding, nine years' weeding'; and how true this is, for most weed seeds will lie dormant in the ground and retain their vitality for a number of years, some for an extraordinary length of time. Fallowing for, say, one growing season will not completely clear the ground of weeds but, assiduously done, it will probably reduce the seed population by up to 50 per cent.

When brought near to the surface these dormant weed seeds will germinate. The essential part of bare fallowing is the frequent cultivation of the ground against any remnants of the perennial weeds and the encouraging of the seeds of others to germinate, destroying the seedlings by the next cultivating process and creating germinating conditions for more seeds thus brought near to the surface. The periods between cultivations must be lengthy enough to allow weed seeds to germinate. If a long drought occurs during this fallowing, one should not be misled by the absence of germinating weeds into assuming that the ground has been cleared of them; they will probably be remaining dormant only through lack of surface moisture. It may even be well worth while giving a thorough watering with a hosepipe to start germination off again.

While it may not always be practical to employ these initial skirmishing tactics, it is never wise to be in too much of a hurry to plant ground which has been cleared and cultivated after having been a breeding place for weeds for a number of years. If fallowing cannot be practised it becomes all the more important to continue the attack relentlessly as soon as necessary after sowing or planting while one can readily operate between the young plants and before insidious weeds penetrate into the hearts of them.

PROPER CONSTRUCTION

Clearing the ground is, as we have seen, one of the most important constructional details, whether in preparing a home for plants or as a basis for the sowing or turfing of a lawn. While turves may put paid to the aspirations of weed sands they will not always prevent the buried roots of docks, dandelions, thistles and other strong perennials from thrusting their shoots up to light and air and continuing their existence.

Even the laying of a hard surface like tar-macadam or concrete may not keep weeds in subjection. Done properly, it should form an impenetrable barrier to even the strongest perennial weed, but if it is put down in a thin layer only, one that is liable to crack at an early date under constant traffic, then such weeds may either find their way through the cracks or seeds will fall into them, germinate and soon gain a foothold in the soil beneath. The ubiquitous annual meadow-grass is noted for its capacity to establish itself in any little crack or cranny.

Cracks in hard surfaces like these not only provide homes for weeds but allow water to enter, turn to ice and expand when the temperature drops. This expansion and subsequent contraction, assisted by the initial establishment of weeds, helps to widen the cracks and to start the disintegration of the surface, especially a tar-macadam one. Treating the ground with a suitable weed-killer before laying tar-macadam is a wise precaution if perennial weeds have had a home there.

Likewise with the cracks between paving slabs or crazy paving. These provide ideal settling places for many weeds and should be made inviolate from the start by adequate grouting in with sand and cement mixture, preferably applied dry when it is easier to fill the crevices thoroughly. With crazy paving it is wise not to abut the pieces too close together, otherwise it will be difficult to get the sand and cement mixture in.

When laying such paving on very weedy ground, one can spare oneself the task of first cleaning it thoroughly, and can effectively prevent any aftergrowth of weeds by simply covering the levelled formation with plastic sheeting and laying the paving directly on this. The plastic sheeting should be preferably of a heavy gauge: old plastic wrappings from bales of peat, or fertiliser bags cut open, are ideal provided there is a good overlap of about 15cm (6in) where the pieces abut. If one wishes to insert paving plants, all that is necessary is to take out suitable pieces of stone before grouting in, filling the spaces with sand or soil for a time or adopting other means to prevent the sand and cement mixture from trickling in, later removing this, then cutting the plastic round the edges of the holes, removing and planting in the soil beneath, or removing this and adding fresh soil if desirable.

When building dry-stone retaining walls, it is highly important to eradicate perennial weeds from the ground behind and to construct in a solid and sound manner so that there are no weaknesses to present opportunities to weeds. Despite all precautions taken during construction a dry-stone wall is a vulnerable object, for soil and not cement is used for bedding between the layers of stone. When a wall supports a weed-ridden bank one can effect a compromise by using cement, taking care that this is not brought too much forward to become visible at the face, thus spoiling the effect. If no through spaces are left for wall plants, there must be an occasional weep-hole through which water can penetrate to prevent its building up behind the wall and exerting pressure.

If, despite all constructional precautions, deep-rooted perennials find their way in or through, they will be extremely difficult to extract. Even annuals with fibrous roots will cling tenaciously and pulling them may result in dislodgement of the stones if no cement has been used and the wall is not soundly constructed. It is therefore very important to oust these weeds before their roots have had time to get a proper grip.

A rock-garden can become a positive breeding place for weeds if the ground is not thoroughly cleaned before the rocks are laid and annuals and other weeds prolific of seed are not removed in good time. Every root beneath or between stones or finding its way into a crevice will be difficult to extract, and the nature of many rock-plants is such that unwelcome strangers in their midst are not easy to dislodge.

THE IMPORTANCE OF GOOD DRAINAGE

A soil which does not drain freely and is in a continual state of moisture above the average suits quite a number of weeds, particularly annuals of quick growth like polygonums, fat hen, chickweed and groundsel. Where it is really wet, almost to the point of being water-logged, buttercups, especially the creeping type, will thrive. So too will the rushes and that deep forager, the horse-tail.

Perhaps even more important is the fact that a wet soil is always more difficult to work. Drawing out the roots of perennial weeds is an exacting business and many pieces may be left behind to grow again. Hoeing will not be easy: one may have to wait a long time for the surface to dry out before it can even be attempted and there will be much more danger of weeds taking root again, especially after even a light shower of rain, following the hoeing operation.

How to drain the soil does not come within the scope of this book, but attention must be drawn to the fact that this aspect of garden formation can be very important to subsequent maintenance. Most garden plants grow better in ground that is reasonably well drained; they are healthier and better able to play their part in denying weeds living room.

ENCOURAGING OPTIMUM GROWTH

Man, animal or plant in full vigour is always in better shape to repel any enemy than when suffering from malnutrition and the side effects of ill-health brought on by other external organisms. Encouraging optimum growth not only leads to a better defence by the individual plant, enabling it to rise and crowd out the invader, but as we shall consider later, it is a great factor in collective security. It should be remembered, however, that optimum growth does not necessarily mean maximum growth. A plant can usually be made to grow large and apparently flourishing by being plied with extra nitrogen, but such growth may well be lush and soft, with the plant liable to flop under its own weight or in a stiff breeze, susceptible to disease and unable to withstand the vicissitudes of winter. Optimum growth means the maximum balanced growth achieved by according a plant the right site and soil conditions and a diet whereby nitrogen is correctly balanced with other nutrients, in particular phosphates and potash in relation to the plant's needs.

CHAPTER SEVEN

MANNING THE DEFENCES

Let us assume that the garden has been constructed in such a way that it is, as far as possible, cleared of all unwanted tenants, designed and made to be less inviting to their return and easier to clear them out again if they re-establish a foothold. We now turn to the rightful occupants, the plants themselves, to do their share in protecting their tenancy.

We have looked at the need to obtain maximum health and growth; but no matter how congenial the soil in general may be, the plants will not flourish if the situation as a whole is not to their liking. We cannot expect the maximum from warmth-loving plants if they are asked to grow in a latitude which is too cold for them in the winter or which is open to strong cold winds at any season of the year. If a plant is an out-and-out sun lover, it will not be so happy if forced to endure a measure of shade; conversely, a plant which likes respite from the scorching summer sun will not thrive in full exposure to its rays. There are in-between requirements to satisfy if maximum growth is to follow.

As for soil, it may not be enough to cultivate it properly, to improve its drainage, its physical nature and its chemical content, if basically, it is wrong for a particular plant or group of plants. To take the extreme, we should not expect good results from rhododendrons, heathers and other acid-soil lovers in a medium which has a naturally high lime content, although attempts are often made to grow them under these conditions and the result is poor, unhealthy, defenceless plants.

If, not withstanding unsuitable soil conditions, one decides to attempt to grow certain plants, one must not be half-hearted in providing them with the medium in which they delight, otherwise the struggle for existence will leave them without the strength to resist competition. While it may be that there are ways and means of overcoming most of the natural difficulties of site and soil, one should certainly avoid overstocking a garden with plants for which the prevailing conditions are not tailor-made, otherwise there will be an increasing risk of a take-over bid by unwanted plants.

PLANTING TO REPEL WEEDS

In a properly planted garden there will be little room for weeds once the rightful occupants have established themselves and attained maturity, at least in those places which can be termed permanently planted. In the parts devoted to the culture of vegetables and fruit there will of course be bare soil visible for much of the season, but given all the space they need for optimum growth, and no more, most of the lower-growing crops will eventually cover the ground to the detriment of weeds. But of course there are crops like peas and runner-beans which grow upwards rather than outwards and which require access room for frequent picking; there are others like onions which have sparse coverage, so one must expect to provide some living room for weeds in this part of the garden.

With fruit, other than soft fruit, once the trees or bushes have become established, the ground beneath can be grassed down or planted with other crops or plants without serious detriment to the fruit; but one should always bear in mind any effect which spraying the fruit against pests and diseases may have, if the plants beneath are edible or constitute permanent groundwork.

Beds and borders devoted to annual floral displays should be so planted that within a reasonable space of time the plants will meet and no bare soil will be visible for the rest of their occupancy. If one cannot afford to plant to achieve this, it is far better to reduce the number or size of the beds or borders or to fill them with more permanent subjects.

REINFORCING ROSES

Rose-beds can be furnished with ground-cover plants to crowd out weeds and to produce some delightful colour effects, but this does make it a little more difficult to carry out the various operations on the roses, such as pruning, fertilising, removing spent blooms and spraying against pests and diseases. A lot depends on the importance placed on roses in the garden and on how meticulously they are cared for. The pruning and spring fertilising programme need not be hampered unduly if short ground-cover plants which die back during the winter are chosen. If these are not likely to be damaged or seriously marred by the application of fungicides to the roses, some of which leave a noticeable deposit on the leaves, all that is then necessary is a little care when one is cutting flowers for indoors or removing spent blooms. If there is a black spot problem with the roses and one tries assiduously to control the disease by removing and burning all fallen rose leaves and by adding winter spraying with a fungicide to the maintenance programme, then ground cover is not really a viable proposition.

NON-ATTENTION HERBACEOUS BORDERS

With herbaceous borders the best effect and best coverage of the ground are obtained when the plants are set out in groups of each kind rather than individually. Planted just a little closer than their maximum spread, the plants in each group should then merge into a solid mass with no bare soil visible. The best overall coverage of a border is obtained when one relies mainly on the bushier, more spreading kinds of plant rather than on the upright growers, with the added advantage that in most cases little or no staking will be required.

For instance, towards the back of the border the tall upright Michaelmas daisies, heleniums, delphiniums and the like can be superseded by the interesting and architectural bear's-breeches, *Acanthus mollis* and *A. spinosus*; the invaluable late-flowering *Anemone* × *hybrida* (*A. hupehensis*, *A. japonica*); and the elegant

Aruncus sylvester (*Spiraea aruncus*). In the middle regions the aromatic bergamot, *Monarda didyma* and its cultivars will grow sturdily, flower over a long period and take over their own patch. The oriental poppy, *Papaver orientalis*, although the stems of which, supporting the large brilliant flowers, may twist a little if wind and heavy rain prevail, has ample foliage to spread over the ground.

The herbaceous peonies, the red-hot pokers (*Kniphofia*) (*Tritoma*) in varying sizes, and the day lilies (*Hemerocallis*) in a wide range of delicate colours and blends, when planted amid somewhat dwarfer subjects to set off their form, will add dignity and character. The dwarfer golden rods like *Solidage* 'Lemore' and 'Golden Mosa', can take the place of the taller kinds. The large basal leaves of *Limonium* (*Statice*) *latifolium* tend to discourage weeds and the great sprays of tiny flowers make invaluable 'everlastings'.

Most of the taller hardy geraniums are bushy and self-supporting. The lavender-blue *Geranium sylvaticum* 'Mayflower' is one of the best for the border, or the deeper tone of *G. grandiflorum* may be preferred. Where the ground is moist the garden astilbes will charm with their plumes of flowers for several weeks, many of the cultivars preceding this display with attractive bronze and reddish tints in their young foliage, foliage which remains an asset and is good ground cover after the flowers are spent.

There should be no room for invaders in the front of the border. Here hummocks of dwarf asters will provide autumn floral colour in the absence of their taller relatives. Erigerons will flower on and off all summer; so too will the cultivars of *Achillea millefolium*, the geums and the herbaceous potentillas. *Euphorbia epithymoides* (*E. polychroma*) will provide a patch of gold in the spring and black-eyed Susan, *Rudbeckia fulgida speciosa* (*R. speciosa, R. newmannii*) or *R.f.s.* 'Goldsturm' in late summer. There can also be the clumps of greyish leaves and the violet-blue flowers of *Veronica incana*; and for the whole of the summer the catmints will provide a continuous display of flowers and perform a weed-suppressing role so thoroughly that they will be mentioned again in this book in this specific capacity.

These are just a few of the more independent herbaceous perennials, independent because they will not require propping up or much fussing around which in itself tends to open up corridors to weeds. Most of them tend to bush out and become as broad as high, denying light and air to weeds if thought is given to the ideal spacing which will enable them to grow shoulder to shoulder.

The same principle can be followed with the shrub border, but whether or not one turns more exclusively to those species whose habit makes them ideal for clothing the ground, the method of planting should always be that of setting them a little less apart than their likely spread. This provides for all individuals in a group to merge; the groups should just meet each other and slightly interlock their growth when at their maximum spread.

One appreciates that, in a small garden, group planting has often to give way to a greater number of individuals in the desire for variety, but the same approach to the objective of ultimately forming a solid but definable mass should be followed, a mass in which few weeds will gain a foothold, let alone thrive.

Obviously, in a shrub border, complete coverage may take several years. While I am not completely averse to trying to shorten the wait for fulfilment with herbaceous borders by planting even closer and while I recognise that by so doing I shall also hasten the day when replanting must be carried out, I am quite opposed to adopting this principle within the more permanent framework of a shrub border. I would much rather bridge the gap by temporarily planting dwarf ground cover between the shrubs to form a weed-repelling carpet. This will not interfere with growth, but it will be gradually engulfed by them and phased out, either by the periodic removal of ground-cover plants as they become in danger of being overgrown by the shrubs, or by allowing the shrubs to obliterate them altogether. Some of the carpeting plants may well continue to flower reasonably well under the deciduous shrubs.

The forefront of any shrub border is the place where weeds flourish best, for there is more light and air and a better chance of the benefit of summer rain. Some people, including professionals, seem to have a fetish about giving a nice tidy finish to the shrub border, taking great care to ensure that the occupants do not transgress outside their domain by shearing them off near the boundary, leaving a trimmed front with a clear strip and gaps in which weeds can flourish just where they will be most prominent.

One can never be quite sure that the shrubs have been so spaced that when they are at their maximum spread they will reach just to the front of the border and not attempt to go beyond it. The answer is not to gauge it just right but to allocate a strip along the front of the border, broadening it out here and there into 'pockets' in which suitable ground-cover plants can be set. These plants will also help to bring the front-line shrubs down to ground level. In this way one gets a better finish to the border, seals off the most obvious place for weeds and is able to grow many interesting and beautiful plants which like the companionship of shrubs.

THE ROCK-GARDEN

In the well-constructed rock-garden the minimum of soil will be exposed, but there will be ample supplies beneath and behind the stones for plants to root into. This is how it is in nature and is why so many true alpines have root systems which appear to be out of all proportion to their top growth. Planting and aftercare should ensure that the interspaces of soil are covered up before the plants start to drape the rocks. Where one creates rather more spacious 'pockets' between the stones for the purpose of culti-vating some of the choicer and less rampant plants – although some of these may be happier in a mere chink between rocks with a good 'larder' behind – the surface of the soil that is exposed can often be covered to advantage with a layer of stone chippings of varying size. This will create a drier, more airy bed for the plant cushions to rest on and will very much discourage the germina-tion of weed seeds.

CLOTHING ODD AREAS

Steep banks, awkward corners, ground beneath trees and any-where where it is difficult to grow plants – if even grass will not

E

succeed or at its best be difficult to mow – need not be breeding grounds for weeds. There are plenty of plants which will thrive in such places and keep all but the most powerful of aliens in complete subjection: I shall be discussing these in more detail later.

If as much thought is given to making a garden a closed shop to weeds as to adorning it with the plants and flowers which delight the eye, by using those plants and flowers as allies there will be a good chance of getting the best of two worlds.

GARDEN HYGIENE

This is not just a golden rule in the fight against pests and diseases; we must look upon garden hygiene as one of the basic principles of defence against weeds. None of these unwelcome plants should be allowed to flourish and seed in odd, unimportant corners or hedge bottoms where otherwise they do not matter. No seeding weeds should be put on the compost heap or be left lying about waiting to be burnt. Even if they are not seeding when they are pulled up, if they are in a sufficiently advanced stage they may hurriedly complete their life cycle before they finally shrivel and die. Groundsel and thistles are notorious for their capacity to do this.

Long grass in the more natural parts of the garden or in odd corners may of itself be of no detriment to appearance, but it can become a breeding ground for weeds, especially the types which can infest a more closely mown lawn. One should always take precautions not to introduce weeds into a clean part of the garden. This can easily be done by carelessness in removing and transporting seeding weeds to the area where they are going to be burnt, and also by transferring soil from ground known to be weed-infested, to another part of the garden where the problem does not exist. If plants, particularly those of a perennial kind, are lifted from ground where creeping weeds are present, every bit of weed-root or rooting stem should be carefully removed before the plants are set elsewhere. Clumps of herbaceous plants may be particularly difficult to clear. If they are heavily weed-infested and wone ishes to retain them, washing all the soil away may make it easier to extract the weeds. When accepting gifts of plants from a friend with a weed-ridden garden, check carefully for the existence of perennial weeds in the root-balls.

*   *   *

The contents of this chapter have been but a brief summary of some of the principles of planting and of care of the garden generally so that there is less invitation to weeds; a prelude to the more deliberate use of plants as ground cover which I shall be dealing with at greater length in the next part of this book.

PART THREE

THE WEED-REPELLING ARMY

From the ordinary principles of planning and planting to ease the burden of weed-control afterwards and to crowd out weeds as much as possible, we now turn to even more positive ways of attempting to achieve the Utopia of a weedless garden. The planting of suitable subjects specifically to cover the ground and deny weeds living space is a very interesting and rewarding subsidiary to the cultivation of the usual garden plants. A wide range of both beautiful and interesting subjects can be drawn in as allies, and if they are employed in the right manner they can add considerably to the appearance and charm of a garden, while functioning in a practical manner by lightening the task of maintenance. That appreciable space in the following chapters is devoted to extolling their virtues and detailing their comparatively modest requirements needs no excusing – there is no better and more satisfying way of achieving the goal.

CHAPTER EIGHT

THE GROUND-COVER THEME

Over the past decade or so 'ground cover' has become quite a household term. In the realm of the professional it has been translated into fact, not always with a lot of imagination and often to the extent of becoming boring, especially with the landscaping of new towns and other major housing developments where the accent is often on very large, square or rectangular or long and narrow, flat expanses of low-growing shrubs like potentillas, hebes, cotoneasters and junipers, or carpeting plants like vincas, ivies, *Pachysandra* and *Hypericum calycinum*, used with monotonous regularity.

The home gardener is now ground-cover conscious but seldom practises it in depth or in such a way that it becomes a colourful and interesting feature of the garden rather than a half-hearted attempt to crowd out weeds. Much has been written about ground cover, but generally concerned with the popular subjects already mentioned, or has been rather too comprehensive and somewhat outside the experience of the home gardener.

It would be wrong to give the impression that one has simply to stick ground-cover plants in and that they will get on immediately with the job of creating a barrier against weeds. A few, it is true, will virtually do this but usually they are the more rampant types which, if not carefully sited, may themselves take on the mantle of weeds eventually.

GROUND PREPARATION

It should be remembered that ground-cover plants are generally destined to stay put for a number of years, during which they will have to grow and remain vigorous if they are not in turn to be overwhelmed by the enemies which they are being employed to keep in subjection. While it may be that very many of them are not at all fastidious and will flourish in most reasonable soils, the extra early vigour resulting from good preparation of the soil will be more than repaid. When they are being employed as the finish to a general planting scheme, the preparation accorded to the major subjects will probably suffice. In all other circumstances it is important that the ground should be well dug, cleared of perennial weeds and enriched where necessary with rotted manure or compost, with plenty of peat for plants which require an acid soil or which revel in humus and moisture. A light dressing, just before planting, of an organic fertiliser such as bonemeal or hoof and horn will also help to give the plants a good start.

PLANTING

Planting can be done at almost any time of the year if the plants are in pots or other containers. Generally I prefer to accord ground-cover shrubs the same treatment as I would those of greater proportions by planting the deciduous ones in autumn or between late winter and early spring, and the evergreens in early April if it has not been possible to get them in at the appropriate time in the autumn, or if the site is exposed to north or east winds during the winter.

The softer ground cover, ie the non-woody or only partially woody subjects, I much prefer to plant in spring. In the main these are the dwarfer, more carpeting, types, some of an evergreen nature; and while they are as tough as nails, it is not to their advantage to subject them to winter's blasts and frost-lifting of the soil before they have established themselves. Moreover, when planting in spring – April is generally the most suitable month – the soil disturbance in the course of planting should put paid to the first batch of weed seeds to germinate, thus giving the ground cover a head start over its rivals and enabling it to begin growing vigorously with the minimum of delay.

DISTANCES APART

These naturally vary according to the subject. Broadly speaking, the majority of the ground-cover shrubs will achieve a spread similar to their height, and as one requires them to interlock eventually, the distance apart should be about 15–25cm (6–10in) less. Among the junipers and cotoneasters in particular there are forms which are much wider than they are high, and others which are quite prostrate and capable of spreading widely over the ground. These can obviously be planted farther apart and optimum distances will be given in the next chapter, when we are looking at species and forms.

Many colonising and carpeting plants are capable of appreciable spread, and here it is a matter of finding a happy balance between a plant's capacity and getting reasonably quick ground coverage. Again speaking in broad terms, those which I shall class as colonisers will require on the average about 45cm (18in) each way and the carpeting plants 30cm (12in), but there will be variations which I shall mention.

The very dwarf mat-forming species, although many are capable of considerable spread, do on the whole require to be planted rather closely at 15–30cm (6–12in) apart to attain quick coverage, for generally they are not able to present much resistance to weeds until they are interlocked.

The clump-forming ground coverers, like the ground-cover shrubs, will in general achieve a spread akin to the height of their foliage – not their flower stems – and on the average this means planting around 30–45cm (12–18in) apart each way, to enable them to close up in reasonable time.

The rampant species, for clothing banks and places where they can be given more rein without entering into competition with other plants in the garden, are somewhat variable in the ultimate extent of their growth. Indeed, one can almost say that there is really no maximum, for the majority will go on spreading and rooting as they go until they reach a natural obstruction or boundary or are otherwise prevented from annexing more territory. Planting distances apart must therefore be dealt with when we look at the species individually.

The planting distances suggested above and those which will be specifically mentioned in the succeeding chapters, are the happy medium between thick planting for the quickest possible effect and a patient wait for the plants to attain their maximum growth. It is well to remember that very close planting is not only more expensive but that the plants will soon be in close competition with each other; and that unless they receive specially invigorating treatment, their effective life may be shortened. This may mean premature and complete exhaustion if they are not lifted, the ground re-cultivated and replanting carried out. Naturally, planting at the maximum distances will incure a longer wait, and the plants will not be an effective weed-barrier until they have covered the ground completely.

POST-PLANTING ATTENTION

Whatever the type or species, there will obviously have to be some assistance given until the plants link up and present a united front. Weeds springing up between the plants will have to be destroyed and prevented from seeding for at least a growing season, for there is really no quick and satisfactory way of installing impregnable defences without a waiting period first. This weed-destruction between the ground-cover shrubs can be carried out by the use of a hoe, by weed-smothering mulches or by recourse to chemical weed-control: all these operations will be dealt with in Part Four of this book.

There is too much risk of damage to the plants if one uses chemicals between the softer forms of ground cover. The contact herbicides will be difficult to apply without splashing the plants and the residual ones may inhibit the outward spread of the ground cover, especially where this is achieved largely by procumbent rooting shoots. Careful hoeing can be carried out for a time after planting, but as these subjects generally are inclined towards surface rooting coupled with spread, I am not in favour of too much disturbance of the surface soil and prefer to change over to weeding by hand the moment I feel that the hoe is becoming a dangerous weapon. Weeding by hand is not usually a particularly onerous task if the ground was well cleared of perennial weeds before planting, and if the planting and post-planting operations of stirring the surface have encouraged weed-seed germination and the early destruction of the resulting seedlings.

Although ground-cover planting, whether with shrubs or with other suitable subjects, is fairly carefree, one must remember that it is a quite intensive method of cropping the ground and is bound to increase the demands on it. Initial improvement and enrichment will not last forever and once the plants have become starved they may tend to degenerate, become less impenetrable and even die out in patches, especially those which are rapid growers and gross feeders. Strength and vitality must be maintained. Nature normally attends to this with fallen leaves and we should try to emulate nature by allowing the annual mulch to remain – both the discarded leaves of the ground-cover plants themselves and those from neighbouring trees – and during the winter, harden our hearts against an ultra-tidy garden, which is not always a thriving and interesting one.

If we remove nature's mulch then we ought to replace it; but I do believe in letting the leaves lie wherever they can be held and hidden by the top growth of the plants. Large tree-leaves lying on top of the carpeting plants must be removed as soon as leaf-fall ceases. These leaves can go on to the compost heap and be returned in due course in the form of an annual mulch up to 25mm (1in) thick, worked in between the plants with the hands, on top of any recently fallen leaves left *in situ*.

If the odd plant dies, one should never wait for the gap to be filled by other plants around unless they are capable of spreading so rapidly that it will be only a very short time before the gap is closed. Every break in the defences will provide a foothold for weeds. A dead shrub should be replaced as soon as practicable and with the low-growing forms of ground cover it is usually a quite simple task to take rooted pieces from the thickest parts, or to lift and divide a clump in the spring to provide material for filling the gaps.

There must be no regular pruning programme for shrubs,

otherwise the object will be defeated. The great majority of the subjects which will be mentioned later in this book require practically no pruning. Dead wood must of course be removed, and where there is some congestion in the top growth it may be beneficial to take out odd branches to enable the rest to remain strong and vigorous. In the early years a little shortening back here and there to encourage bushiness may be desirable, or in later years to help thin places to fill in. Odd straggling growths may need cutting back to promote bushiness at the base.

Some forms of ground cover like vincas, pachysandras, *Geranium macrorrhizum* and bergenias need practically no other attention. Others require little more than a cleaning out of the decaying leaves still attached, just before growth starts in the spring. *Hypericum calycinum*, epimediums and *Ceratostigma* will benefit from cutting back with shears at the same time. *Tellima*, *Brunnera*, pulmonarias and some of the geraniums are improved by the removal of the old flower-stems as they fade: this helps a resurgence of foliage growth. Hostas, *Nepeta*, *Alchemilla* and others are herbaceous and need the annual removal of old growth, preferably after the worst of the winter is over. These are just examples: one soon learns what is the minimal treatment necessary to keep each species tidy and to prevent it from becoming congested with dead or useless growth.

REPLANTING

This will not be a regular routine. Shrubs will of course go on until they become old and decrepit. The mats of ivy, *Hypericum calycinum*, vincas and *Pachysandra*, the colonies of *Euphorbia robbiae*, *Geranium macrorrhizum* and lily-of-the-valley, and the groups of *Galax*, hostas and epimediums will continue unperturbed for a number of years if they are not left completely to fend for themselves. But with ajugas, *Houttuynia*, *Polygonum affine* and *Mentha* there is a tendency for the centres of the mats or colonies to become worn out after several years; and with some of the clump-forming plants there comes a time when they need to be reinvigorated by lifting, having their larder replenished and replanting.

Usually it is just a matter of doing a little renovation here and there as the need arises. This requires no great effort and little or no expense, for in general more than enough material for re-planting will become available. Indeed, one need have no qualms about bringing forward some of the replanting, if one is in need of stock for extending the ground cover to other parts of the garden. This work, as with initial planting, is best done in the spring.

BANK PLANTING

Perhaps the great majority of the subjects we shall be looking at shortly adapt themselves very well to clothing banks where other forms of planting are either costly or difficult to establish, and where grass is far from easy to keep mown. Where the bank is particularly steep, the initial problem with ground cover may well be the erosion of the soil after it has been cultivated and prepared for planting. This is where the more rampant subjects come in useful, especially those with the capacity to cover large areas individually. Requiring much wider spacing, they can be planted with no more disturbance to the bank than the excavation of a hole, rather larger than usual, for each plant. If desirable, the soil can be improved or replaced. The rest of the bank can remain undisturbed, but it will be necessary to destroy all weed and grass growth beforehand with chemicals, using a paraquat type of weed-killer which does not poison the soil, coupled with a selective weedkiller for the deep-rooted perennials. More details about these methods will be given later in this book.

In the chapters which follow I shall concentrate on plants which are not too difficult to obtain, although one may occasionally have to go to one of the larger nurseries, or to a firm specialising in ground cover, if they are not available at a local Garden Centre. There are many other plants which are eminently suitable for the purpose of ground cover but it would be of little avail to bring their virtues to light if they are likely to be beyond the reach of those for whom this book is intended.

CHAPTER NINE

GROUND-COVER SHRUBS

Whereas the landscape gardener may use one individual species or cultivar in some depth, the home gardener will naturally want more variety in the much smaller space at his disposal. He must however still think in terms of group planting as much as possible otherwise he will partially defeat his object, for plants of one kind tend to establish a closer unity than is usually achieved by mixed planting. Generally, three is the minimum number for forming a well-shaped group but there is no reason why the odd single specimen, preferably rather broader and taller than those around, should not be inserted here and there to introduce variety and to break up any tendency towards flatness and formality.

The quite prostrate shrubs must naturally be placed in the front of a bed, round it or occupying a corner or an outjutting position. Nowhere do they look better than when they are covering a slope or draping themselves over the front of a raised border. Their ability to occupy a lot of ground must be taken into account, otherwise they may soon transgress beyond the boundary where border meets grass or path.

LOW-GROWING COTONEASTERS

Of the spreading forms, the well-known *Cotoneaster horizontalis*, whose flattened, herring-bone branching system is so often employed to cover a low wall, in the open ground will eventually cover an area exceeding 2m (6ft) in diameter, but the shrubs should preferably be planted no farther apart than this to obtain quick, dense ground cover. There is a form called 'Variegatus' which has pleasing silver-variegated foliage, but as it is not so vigorous as the type, it must be planted more closely. *C. micro-phyllus* has a similar spread, but it lacks the attractive network form of *C. horizontalis* and is inclined to be less dense in habit. It is an evergreen. So too is *C. congestus* which, being confined in spread and more mound-like in character, can often be used where the other forms are too broad.

Among the several prostrate cotoneasters, *C. dammeri* (*C. humifusus*) grows and forms a carpet probably little more than 10cm (4in) high. A form of this, called 'Coral Beauty', has very attractive coral-red fruits. *C. salicifolius* 'Repens' has willow-like foliage and is a strong low spreader. Then there are *C.* 'Saldam', a hybrid between *C. dammeri* and *C. salicifolius* and another hybrid, *C.* 'Skogholm', which is becoming very popular.

All these are evergreens, although they may lose some of their leaves in a hard winter. *C. dammeri* can be planted about 1m (3½ft) apart, a little more if one is willing to wait for it to spread its carpet, while *C. salicifolius* 'Repens', *C.* 'Saldam' and *C.* 'Skogholm' require a little more space in which to manoeuvre.

THE DWARF HEBES

Most of the hebes, which used to be called *Veronica*, make good, bushy, evergreen flowering shrubs. The pick of the dwarfer ones with good ground-covering capacity are *Hebe anomala* and *H. rakaiensis* (*H. subalpina* of gardens) with small bright green and apple-green foliage respectively and a mass of white flowers in late summer. The former makes bushes around 1m (3½ft) high, while *H. rakaiensis* is somewhat dwarfer. Both require rather more space than their height.

H. 'Autumn Glory' grows about 45cm (18in) high only and in late summer has violet-blue flowers which contrast well with the copper-tinted foliage. *H.* 'Carl Teschner' is paler in the tone of its flowers which have a pleasing white throat for contrast and are produced rather earlier in the summer on compact, but quite free-growing, low bushes with a spread of about 60cm (24in).

H. pinguifolia 'Pagei' (*H. pageana*) with white flowers in May and June, and *H. pimeleoides* 'Glaucocoerulea' with lavender flowers in June and July, have glaucous grey and glaucous blue foliage respectively. The former at about 30cm (12in) high is the shorter of the two. Both, when planted about 45cm (18in) apart, will form a complete low mat over the ground.

All these hebes require little or no attention, except that *H.* 'Autumn Glory' will benefit by having its taller, more straggling growths cut back in the spring to induce new ones from the base and keep it close and compact.

THE SPREADING POTENTILLAS

A whole host of the shrubby, deciduous potentillas will flower continuously throughout the summer and make excellent spreading bushes requiring practically no attention. Many of them are cultivars and hybrids of *Potentilla fruticosa* and one can almost choose at will, so I shall select just one each of the most spreading kinds in a range of colours. For white, it would be *mandschurica*, 45cm (18in) high × 75cm (30in) wide; for primrose-yellow, 'Primrose Beauty', 90cm (36in) × 1·2m (4ft), with the deep yellow 'Klondyke' and the orange 'Tangerine', both 75cm (30in) × 1·2m (4ft). The last named keeps its colour better when growing in partial shade. Then I must add one taller and very fine cultivar, the light yellow hybrid *P.* 'Elizabeth', 90cm (36in) × 1·5m (4ft), one of the densest in growth and most prolific of flower.

SOME COLONISING SHRUBS

The great favourite is the Oregon grape, *Mahonia aquifolium*, which well deserves its popularity. That it has become slightly commonplace should not deter anyone from planting it, for its handsome evergreen foliage will look well in sun or shade and assume purplish-bronze tints in the winter, especially when it has had its fair share of sun. Its cultivar 'Atropurpurea' is even more richly coloured at that season. Then there are the short, dense, upright racemes of sweetly scented flowers opening as early as the end of February, followed by black berries which make a pleasant blackcurrant-like jam. Plant about 60cm (24in) apart for quick coverage and cut any long straggling stems hard back after flowering to encourage the formation of a thick 1m (3½ft) high mass.

Perhaps it is against a wall that the flowering quinces, formerly *Cydonia* and now *Chaenomeles*, show off their flowers to the best advantage; but they are also first-rate free-standing shrubs. Several of the numerous cultivars are inclined to be sprawling, none more so than *C.* × *superba* 'Crimson and Gold' with an overall height of around 1·5m (5ft), a width somewhat greater, and a capacity to sucker as it spreads and to form a real thicket.

The snow-berries, *Symphoricarpos*, are also suckering subjects. Always popular for their large white fruits, rose-pink in 'Magic Berry' and pink-tinted in 'Mother-of-Pearl', in general they are subjects for planting where they can be given some latitude, and they are excellent for shady places. For the smaller garden the newer pink-fruited *S.* × *chenaultii* 'Hancock' is probably the best bet. It is little more than 60cm (24in) high, is a good spreader and will soon make a twiggy mass when planted 1m (3½ft) or so apart.

The best ground-covering roses are to be found among the vigorous climbing kinds when relegated to sprawling over the ground, and these are most suitable for banks. *Rosa nitida* is, however, a dwarf suckering species capable of forming a low thicket about 45cm (18in) high with scented pink flowers, bright red hips and exceptionally bright red autumn foliage. Plant it between 60cm (24in) and 90cm (36in) apart.

TONES OF SILVER AND GREY

Shrubs with silver or grey foliage are always acceptable in a garden provided they are not overdone. They are of particular value during the winter for contrasting with the darker evergreens. *Hebe pinguifolia* 'Pagei' and *H. pimeleoides* 'Glaucocoerulea' have already been mentioned. Then of course there is the ever popular lavender. Although they do have to be planted more closely, I prefer the dwarf compact forms like *Lavandula* 'Hidcote' and *L.* 'Folgate', or the rather taller so-called Dutch lavender *L.* 'Vera', to the common and other taller kinds which become sprawling and woody more rapidly. This gauntness may be due in part to a reluctance to trim back the shrubs quite severely with the shears after flowering. I prefer to do this in two stages: a light

Page 81 (*above*) Heathers en masse are first-rate ground coverers; (*below*) *Viburnum davidii* – attractive, corrugated evergreen foliage and white flowers succeeded by violet berries

Page 82 (above) *Geranium macrorrhizum* and bergenias provide foliage contrast in the author's garden; (below) the dwarf Russian comfrey, *Symphytum grandiflorum*, a weed suppressor in shady places

trim over to tidy them up for the winter and a further shortening back in spring. It is advisable to begin fairly severe pruning at a quite early stage and not to wait until the shrubs are approaching the maximum dimensions required.

I must admit to some confusion as to whether *Senecio greyi* masquerades under *S. laxifolius* or vice versa, but whatever is commonly sold under either name is a first-class, spreading, silver-foliaged evergreen now very well known. At around 75cm (30in) high, it is ideal for the front of a shrub border, for obtaining pleasing effects with others of deeper foliage-tone or with contrasting flowers. It produces masses of yellow flowers, sometimes rather haphazardly, and like *Mahonia aquifolium* is all the better if its taller, straggling shoots are cut fairly hard back in spring to maintain bushiness.

The lavender cotton, *Santolina chamaecyparissus*, is a really dwarf, silver-foliaged shrub; it is much better when treated like an herbaceous perennial and trimmed to the ground each spring. Left to its own devices it tends to sprawl out from the centre and become ragged. This trimming may reduce the yellow flowers to a minimum but I always feel that the foliage is far more valuable. With this close cropping each clump will soon form a dense annual hummock some 45cm (18in) high and across. *S. neapolitana* is very similar but it is by no means as compact in growth.

Dorycnium hirsutum is more of a sub-shrub, for its branches die back each winter and are replenished from the base. It makes a charming frontal subject for a shrub border or it can be grown in larger groups. Cut down to the base each spring it soon sends out strong shoots which reach a height of around 60cm (24in) and are clothed with small, woolly, grey-green leaves surmounted by tufts of pink and white pea-shaped flowers from midsummer onwards, followed by small, attractive, reddish-brown fruit-pods. The long growths with their foliage and with either flowers or fruit are exceptionally good for use in flower arranging. This shrub does like a fairly light soil and a sunny position.

Euonymus fortunei radicans 'Variegatus' is capable of forming a solid 40cm (16in) high mat of trailing stems. It is not exceptionally rapid in spreading sideways and is best planted about 60cm (24in) apart to obtain reasonably quick coverage. *E.f.* 'Silver Queen' is

F

somewhat taller and broader. Both shrubs are silver-variegated, excellent for shade and also good in sun when their foliage will become tinged with pink in winter. At that season their warm and bright colour is to be valued greatly.

HEATHS AND THEIR ALLIES

The great majority of the dwarfer heaths, given the right conditions and spacing, will cover the ground with a weed-repelling mat. I will isolate a few which are outstanding in this respect. The winter-flowering groups are the most valuable for they are lime-tolerant; but if the pH of the soil is rather high, plenty of peat should be added to make it more suitable. Among the cultivars of the mountain heath, *Erica carnea*, both 'Springwood White' and 'Springwood Pink' are exceptionally good and 'Foxhollow Fairy', a very pretty form with flowers opening white and turning to pink, is also a quite vigorous trailer. The winter-flowering hybrids in general are also robust and spreading, especially *E.* × *darleyensis* and its forms 'Arthur Johnson', 'George Rendall', 'Furzey' (identical with 'Cherry Stevens') and 'Silberschmelze' ('Silver Beads').

Next to the winter-flowering heaths, the Cornish heath, *E. vagans* and its cultivars are probably the most accommodating, for generously supplied with peat they will not object to a soil which is slightly alkaline. For quick ground cover one should choose the most vigorous cultivars like 'Cream', 'Rubra' and 'Grandiflora'.

Among the garden forms of the common ling, *Calluna vulgaris*, 'Foxhollow Wanderer' will be found to be excellent for the purpose of ground cover, and the slightly taller 'Joan Sparkes' is also very useful. The Dorset heath, *Erica ciliaris*, also tends to be of trailing habit and does not object to partial shade, which most heaths dislike. Its most vigorous cultivar is 'Camla', which is quite late in producing its purplish-pink flowers but continues right into November. The latter should not be confused with *Calluna vulgaris* 'Camla' which is a synonym for *C.v.* 'County Wicklow'. Although not quite so vigorous, *Erica ciliaris* 'Wych' also forms wide mats and flowers over a long period.

Despite the desire to get quick coverage, I consider it folly to plant heaths really close. It is true that a well-nigh impenetrable mat is soon formed, but the internal competition engendered does tend to shorten the lives of the plants and lower the quality of their flowers. Given full spacing – and this can mean as much as 90cm (36in) apart for the strongest and widest growers – the hummocky effect created is much more inviting than a solid, level mass. But planting at the maximum distance apart does require time before the plants meet and one must therefore find distances between this and the ultra-close planting which is too often practised. As a general guide I would say around 45cm (18in) for the more compact, bushy kinds and up to 75cm (30in) for the really strong spreaders like the winter-flowering hybrids.

One should not neglect to give these heaths a trim over with the shears after flowering. This does assist them to make dense growth and to produce better flowers. It is particularly important with *E. ciliaris* 'Camla and' *E. vagans* 'Grandiflora', which are inclined to become leggy and loose if left alone. With the summer-flowering kinds I like to leave this trimming until early spring, for the dead flowers have much attraction during the winter months, especially the russet-brown spikes of *E. vagans* and its cultivars.

Turning now to a couple of allies of the heath, ie genera of the same family requiring similar acid-soil conditions, there is much winter joy in the large white, pink or red berries of *Pernettya mucronata*. The 'Davis' Hybrids' are an excellent strain and will make a close thicket 60–90cm (24–36in) high. Although self-fertile the pernettyas always fruit better when they are planted in groups.

In shade, even if the soil tends to become dry beneath trees, the vigorous evergreen shallon, *Gaultheria shallon* with white, bell-shaped flowers and purple berries beloved by pheasants, will make a thicket 90cm (36in) or more in height when the shrubs are planted a similar distance apart. While it may not be a particularly choice shrub, it is certainly useful where there is space beneath trees to clothe.

SPREADING AND PROSTRATE JUNIPERS

These are superb for ground cover on a large scale, but for the small garden it is a little difficult to decide what to recommend.

They are of a wide-spreading nature, some of them rooting as they go, and this gives them the capacity to continue spreading indefinitely. Their growth rate, however, is not really rapid – up to about 15cm (6in) per year – which means that if one takes their ultimate outward dimensions too much into account one will have to wait a long time for them to link up. They are not cheap, so one cannot afford to pack them in for quick effects. Unless therefore one has a fair amount of space to devote to them they may have to be used in small groups only, sometimes singly. Indeed, when they are planted in this way they can be very effective, especially when they are able to trail over the edge of a low wall or rockwork, or down a slope. The prostrate ones are ideal for clothing banks, given time to do so.

I suggest, therefore, that it is best to try to find some happy compromise in their use, ie if planting them singly or in very small groups, give them rather more room and fill in between with suitably low carpeting plants as temporary weed-suppressors. When they are planted in broader masses, they can be closed up somewhat for quicker overall coverage.

Working on this principle the spreading kinds can be given about 1·8m (6ft) spacing down to 90cm (36in), and the prostrate ground-huggers a little extra. They are all capable of more than filling this space, but it will take quite a few years for them to do so.

Numerous low-growing junipers will be found listed in books dealing with conifers, and in many cases one could choose any of several and be equally satisfied. Not all, however, are readily available but there should be no difficulty in obtaining any of the following.

Among those which make wide, flat-topped bushes, *Juniperus sabina tamariscifolia* is the most common of the green types and at about 60cm (24in) high is rather dwarfer than *J.* × *media* 'Pfitzerana'. The golden form of the latter, called 'Pfitzerana Aurea' is good, although it tends to turn more of a yellowish-green in the winter, but its sport, 'Old Gold' retains its colour better and is rather more compact. *J.* 'Grey Owl' is a most attractive form with grey-blue foliage.

The prostrate junipers are eminently suitable for clothing banks, but because of their comparatively slow rate of growth

they cannot be included with the rampant ground coverers described in a later chapter. *J. communis* 'Hornibrookii' has green
leaves which are silver beneath. *J.c.* 'Repanda' is also green but
becomes tinted with brown in winter. Both *J. horizontalis* 'Bar
Harbour' and the Waukegan juniper, *J.h.* 'Douglasii' are more
grey-green, becoming purplish in winter. *J.h.* 'Glauca', as its
name implies, has blue-green foliage. None of these prostrate
forms are likely to exceed 30cm (12in) in height, and all of them
make most attractive spreading mats.

MORE USEFUL EVERGREENS

While the common laurel, *Prunus laurocerasus*, is outside the scope
of this book, it has several low-growing forms which have become
extremely popular for wide planting effects. 'Zabelliana', with
very narrow leaves, is quite a spreader but the new 'Otto Luyken'
is more suitable for a small garden as it is dwarfer – about 1·2m
(4ft) high ultimately but it can easily be kept lower – and rather
more compact. Moreover, it has claims to be quite a good-class
flowering shrub with its upright racemes of white flowers in June.

Viburnum davidii, with rounded, corrugated leaves, has also
made a name for itself as a ground-cover shrub. It has a neat,
rounded habit, is about 60cm (24in) high and rather more across,
and although its white flowers in June are not very exciting, they
are followed by turquoise-blue berries if several shrubs are
planted together for cross-pollination.

Winter flowers on shrubs are often rather inconspicuous, but
often very fragrant. This is so with the comparatively modest
Sarcococca humilis, a neat 60cm (24in) high suckering shrub for
filling in the front of a shrub border, particularly in the shady
parts. It is a low solid mass of shining evergreen leaves from which
the delightful fragrance of the rather insignificant white flowers
is wafted during the late winter.

BARBERRIES AND OTHERS

For thorny barriers where such are desirable one cannot go far
wrong with barberries, and they are excellent in their own right.

There is a wide choice, but for the purpose in mind I would select *Berberis candidula*, the thicket-forming *B. calliantha*, together with *B. verruculosa*, all of which are evergreens; and of the deciduous kinds, *B. wilsoniae* and its cultivars. The first and the last named grow about 90cm (36in) high, the others around the 1·2m (4ft) mark. All are somewhat broader than high and none of them is particularly fast growing, but all are extremely good for making dense, impenetrable masses with very little attention.

In nature the common gorse takes over large tracts of land, and despite its ubiquity it is always admired when in full golden bloom and for its readiness to break out into flower again spasmodically at any other season of the year, including the winter months. It is not, however, really a subject for the smaller garden, not even the dwarfer double-flowered form; but we can turn to its near relative, the Spanish gorse, *Genista hispanica*, whose intensely spiny, dense, formal hummocks are wreathed with gold in May and June. To become effective without too much delay, it needs to be planted about 75 cm (30in) apart to create a barrier not likely to be breached by plant or animal.

Its kinsman, *G. lydia*, very similar in flower but quite different in growth and habit, forms a mass of arching, practically unarmed shoots. Both are subjects for full sun and are ideal for light, even dry and hungry soils. So too are their near relatives, the brooms, among which the very dwarf – no more than 30cm (12in) high – sprawling masses of *Cytisus* × *kewensis* (sulphur-yellow) and *C.* × *beanei* (golden-yellow) are excellent for patches in the rock-garden, for draping banks and for forming low ground cover in the very front of a shrub border.

Lastly, there is a great favourite of mine whose true potential is now being realised. *Lonicera pileata* is a bush honeysuckle not unlike the popular hedging plant *L. nitida*, except that it is low-growing and spreads out horizontally. It has small, bright green, semi-evergreen foliage, with rather inconspicuous flowers but attractive violet-coloured berries. Given about 1m (3½ft) each way, it soon forms a flat but not at all inelegant or monotonous canopy over the ground, of similar height to its spread or a little less.

*   *   *

The plants I have described in this chapter are by no means all the low-growing species and cultivars of shrubs available for planting as ground cover. Confined though this selection may be, it is still large enough and wide enough to impart considerable variety, whether or not it is backed up by the taller, perhaps more glamorous, sorts.

CHAPTER TEN

COLONISING PLANTS

It could of course be said that true ground cover is the act of colonising plants. These are plants that extend, merge and fully occupy the ground, not simply spreading their top growth over it. The same capacity, but to a less dominating degree, is possessed by many of the dwarfer carpeting species which will be discussed later.

A few of these spreaders, rooting as they go, may tend to transgress beyond the territory allotted to them, but they are not avid marauders in that they can usually be readily checked when they reach their boundaries. Some are ideal for background planting or for the less delectable spots where a certain amount of vigour and a tight defence are needed; all are, perhaps, best suited by a place in the more natural parts of a garden but most will also occupy a frontal seat with dignity.

A POPULAR TRIO

The rose of Sharon, *Hypericum calycinum*, really needs no description. It will colonise the ground effectively with foliage to a height of 30cm (12in), surmounted by large golden flowers with their prominent bosses of stamens. It is evergreen to the extent that it will retain most of its leaves throughout a normal winter, but although it is a true shrub, it pays dividends to treat it as a sub-shrub by shearing it to the base in early spring.

The periwinkles have likewise established themselves as sure and easy ground cover. Theirs is a capacity for stems to root as they come into contact with the soil, rather than to spread below ground level. With the strong, 40cm (14in) high *Vinca major* and its variegated form 'Elegantissima' ('Variegata'), this secondary rooting and filling in can be speeded up by bending over the longest growths and pinning them to the ground with pegs or pieces of stones. These robust forms require more care in placing and do not form quite such a neat low cover as does *V. minor* and its cultivars, among which one can select 'Alba' with white flowers instead of the periwinkle-blue of the type and of *V. major*, 'Bowles Variety' with larger, deeper blue flowers, and 'Variegata' ('Argentea Variegata') with silver-variegated foliage and a slightly less vigorous habit. There are others but these are among the best variations from the type.

The third in the trio is not so well known, at least by the home gardener. *Pachysandra terminalis* is a shiny-leaved evergreen growing up to around 30cm (12in) in height. It is not at all quick to get going, but it will form a thick and attractive low mass. It has white, very inconspicuous, but scented flowers in February and March; and there is a rather brighter silver-variegated form called 'Variegata' which is slower than the type to establish itself.

MORE SHINING EVERGREENS

The great elephant-ear leaves of the bergenias are to be seen in many a garden. This is a plant with no off period and no particular likes or dislikes: it is happy in sun or shade, in moist or dry ground. It not only has impressive foliage throughout the year but with some of the forms this turns to rich shades of burnished red and maroon for the winter, especially if the plant has had a fair amount of summer sun. The flowers, appearing from early March until May according to the species or cultivar, have a great deal of quality. *Bergenia cordifolia* is the most common species, at its best with its form 'Purpurea'. Others which are especially good for winter foliage are 'Ballawley', 'Profusion', 'Sunningdale' and the dwarf compact 'Abendglut' ('Evening Glow'). All these have flowers in shades of pink; and for a complete change there is 'Silberlicht' ('Silver Light') with white flowers. All the bergenias can be relied upon to close up and form masses of heavy but classical foliage which weeds seldom penetrate; they will do so with next to no attention and go on, apparently unperturbed, for many a year.

The asarabacca, *Asarum europaeum*, likes shade and a moist soil, where it will spread by means of its creeping rootstock and form a quite dense, shining cover 20–30cm (8–12in) high. Its flowers are curious rather than beautiful: brown, three-cleft and tucked away beneath the foliage.

Any plant which will flourish in any soil wet or dry, in sun or in the dense dry shade around the trunks of trees, or will grow up and thrust its way through a privet hedge, yet be very attractive in its own right, is worth consideration for any garden. The danger with such a plant is that there is a chance of its travelling where it should not: *Euphorbia robbiae* is inclined to do this, but it is not difficult to curb. The glossy evergreen leaves are arranged in rosettes on the 45–60cm (18–24in) high stems, which at the apex produce erect panicles of eye-catching greenish-yellow bracts surrounding the inconspicuous flowers. These make their first move long before winter is past, reach their peak in the spring, pass on to pleasant green for several weeks and then gradually turn to straw-yellow.

AROMATIC MASSES

So often have I extolled its virtues, both in writing and in conversation, that I now feel I am singing my swan-song when I mention *Geranium macrorrhizum*. I am always surprised at how few people really know it and at the fewer still who employ and enjoy it. Throughout the summer, its tidy 30cm (12in) high undulating mass of bright green foliage that is full of texture and quality, is smooth and consoling to the eye. The pink flowers – or white in the form 'Album' – sit just above the foliage in June, and when they fade they do not have to be removed for they are swallowed up by the still expanding leaves. But to me the greatest charm is the alluring fragrance of the foliage when it is brushed against: the scent clings to the hands even after washing and to the clothes for hours after.

I also like the habit of the upright permanent stems: a small topmost boss of the youngest leaves remains green on each stem throughout the winter, the stems collecting and retaining all but the largest of the falling autumn leaves to mulch and help sustain the plants. Planted 30–40cm (12–16in) apart, it will fill up in the first season. It will spread outwards but at no great pace and I know of several large drifts that I planted fifteen or more years ago which have remained vigorous and healthy without any attention and have never become percolated with weeds. This to me is ground cover par exellence, especially when it thrives in moist or dry soil, in sun or complete shade.

The variegated form of the round-leaved or apple mint, *Mentha rotundifolia*, now correctly called *M. suaveolens*, is not such a closely knit, tidy plant. It can flop about, it has a tendency to wax strong round the outside and decline in the middle of each colony and it needs occasional lifting, dividing and replanting; but its silver-variegated woolly leaves, with occasional all-white shoots, help to form some delightful contrasts in the ground-cover network.

MORE STEADY SPREADERS

One could label the dwarf Russian comfrey, *Symphytum grandiflorum*, quietly invasive were it not that its tendencies to wander can be checked readily. The large hoary foliage standing about 30cm (12in) above the ground is pretty well evergreen. It is produced from prostrate stems which enable the plants to close the gaps quickly when planted 45cm (18in) apart, and it forms a complete weed-suppressing cover even in the densest shade. This subject is ideal for planting among shrubs and for places where rough but not uncomely verdure is required. At the same time it should not be tucked right away, for there is a lot of charm in the little tubular flowers held just above the foliage in spring; they are creamy yellow in colour and tipped with red before they are fully open.

Many wild plants have improved forms which have become valued garden plants, eg the bistort or snakeweed, *Polygonum bistorta*, is a European native whose garden form, 'Superbum', can be quite delightful, particularly where the soil conditions are on the moist side. From its large, 30cm (12in) long radical leaves, short dense spikes of pink flowers on 90cm (36in) high stems appear in May. Planted some 45cm (18in) apart, the plants soon merge into a dense weed-suppressing colony. Unfortunately, the plant is completely deciduous, but this does not reduce its efficiency or its charm.

The leopard's-bane, *Doronicum*, is not a fully credited ground-covering subject, but my early memories of great colonies of it flourishing as a garden outcast in woodlands make me regard it as just as valuable for this purpose as when flowering in early isolation in a formal herbaceous border. I suppose this particular one was *D. plantagineum*, but the dwarfer modern cultivars like 'Miss Mason' and the double *D. caucasicum* 'Spring Beauty' might also be taken away from the formal border to perform a supporting role elsewhere.

It is a pity that the large violet heads of *Campanula glomerata dahurica* ('Superba') on 30cm (12in) high leafy stems are not produced at the same time, for this plant could then be set in association with the gold of the *Doronicum*. It is a persistent spreader, but controllable. It certainly does take possession of its own patch: like the *Doronicum* it requires little more than the removal of the flowering stems when spent, and it goes on for a number of years before it needs to be reinvigorated by being lifted and replanted.

The common name of leadwort does nothing to enhance the image of *Ceratostigma plumbaginoides* (*Plumbago larpentae*); and this plant is perhaps not so well known in gardens as is the taller, rather more shrubby *C. willmottianum*. It has, however, a similar perfection of tone in the deep, clear blue of its flowers, which are produced in heads at the end of its annual growths just when the foliage is beginning to take on its rich red autumnal tints. More sub-shrub than shrub, it needs to be trimmed to the base each year, and this maintains it at a height of around 30cm (12in). It spreads and colonises by means of underground stems, but it cannot in any sense be termed rampant.

Unlike the *Ceratostigma* which prefers a light, well-drained soil and a sunny position, that immigrant from Japan, *Houttuynia cordata* has more of a penchant for shade and moisture at its feet. Given these conditions, its ability to extend by underground stems may have to be watched; but if its immediate neighbours are shrubs taller than its 30cm (12in) high stems or have their own defences, then its tendency to wander can be kept in check or need cause little concern. The heart-shaped leaves, blotched and pervaded with maroon, show off the four white bracts which surround each cone of inconspicuous true flowers. Its double-flowered form, 'Flora Plena', is rather more attractive, but equally expansive.

The ability to spread outwards as well as within their own territory is, of course, bound to occur with any of these colonising plants. This has to be taken into account when one is choosing sites for them: make sure that they are given neighbours which will not be unduly inconvenienced by any such pressures. Once this precaution has been taken, there really is no need to fear that the plants will ever become invasive to the extent that their image becomes almost as tarnished as that of the weeds they are intended to suppress.

CHAPTER ELEVEN

CARPETING PLANTS

We turn now to those plants which by reason of the natural spread of their growth, or by rooting and colonising as they extend, can form a quite low carpet over the ground. I shall exclude for the time being those plants of even dwarfer stature which we shall consider later as groundwork for the very dwarf bulbs as well as for their capacity to keep down the majority of the usual annual weeds. These somewhat taller carpeting plants also make an ideal base for bulbous subjects more of medium height such as the snake's-head fritillary, *Fritillaria meleagris*; the taller hybrids of *Narcissus cyclamineus* and *N. triandrus*; some of the tulip species; alliums like *Allium ostrowskianum* and *A. moly*; *Anemone apennina*; and where the soil is light and the position warm and sunny, the harlequin flower, *Sparaxis*. Generally I would be very cautious about planting the majority of the taller, heavier garden cultivars of narcissus and tulips among such carpeting plants, for after flowering their foliage persists for some time and may not help or add to the appearance of the ground cover during that period.

Generally these carpeting plants are suitable for the very fore-front of a border devoted to shrubs and hardy plants, bringing it down to the level of the bordering lawn or path. Ideal for very narrow borders where there is a constant weed problem, they can be used to edge off an herbaceous border, as ground cover or as edgings to rose-beds, and for furnishing many an odd corner where taller plants are either out of place or are too confined to make full use of any weed-excluding properties they may possess.

With plants of this nature, which vary somewhat in the way they spread out, ie either by rooting as they go or by merely extending their mat of growth, it is always difficult to advocate

96

common planting distances. Unless otherwise stated, however, one cannot go far wrong if, for reasonably quick coverage, one thinks in terms of about 25cm (10in) apart for the steady colonisers and up to 40cm (16in) for the spreaders and for those which are more vigorous.

These may be parts of a rock-garden where fairly vigorous spreaders are to be preferred to the choicer alpines; or merely slopes in the garden which are too difficult to grass down and mow and where, perhaps, a certain amount of stone has been inserted, not so much with the idea of forming a true rocky bank but for the purpose of supporting the soil and creating a type of semi rock-garden feature. Some of these subjects will do equally well on the flat, but generally they look more at home and are much more effective where there is some contour in the surface.

Among the numerous commoner rock-garden subjects, there are plenty of vigorous, spreading habit; but I will pass by aubretias, arabis, dwarf phloxes, mossy saxifrages and the like and turn to a few others which can be put to a wider use by being employed specifically as ground cover, on the flat as well as on more undulating sites. Needless to say, any of these spreading rock-garden type subjects are also ideal for draping over stones and for furnishing dry-stone walls.

Campanula carpatica and *C. portenschlagiana* (*C. muralis*) and their forms will do the job in a tidy and unobtrusive way, but if one wants something rather assertive then *C. poscharskyana* may be just the thing. This is a real trailer, a little apt to become invasive if it gets half a chance, and it ought to have either definite, inviolate boundaries or neighbours which will not be overrun. It will then do a good job with its evergreen mat of foliage, which becomes covered with a sheet of lavender-blue flowers in late summer.

The mountain avens, *Dryas octopetala*, is a native plant which now has a valued place in the garden. It is not a rapid spreader, but it consolidates itself firmly as it goes on, forming a low, rooting mat of crinkled evergreen leaves which bear in May and June rather chaste white flowers with yellow centres, not unlike miniature single roses. My experience is that these flowers are not put forth in abundance, but this may be because I have grown the plant only in localities where clay is the influencing soil factor, and it really prefers a soil that is better drained.

Very many plants have blue flowers, but only a proportion are a good, clear mid-blue without a hint of lavender, mauve or purple. For this alone *Lithospermum diffusum* (*L. prostratum*), with its good cultivars, 'Grace Ward' and 'Heavenly Blue', has become a valuable rock-garden subject; but it can also be put to the rather more humble task of providing a low carpet of evergreen foliage in places where this is appropriate and where the sheets of deep sky-blue flowers in early summer will be seen and appreciated fully. It does require a lime-free soil, and while it does best in full sun, it will not object to a partially shaded position.

Silver foliage in a garden, provided it is not overdone, is usually a great asset, especially during the winter months when it can do so much to brighten the picture. One can have broad carpets of it with *Artemisia stellerana* trailing over walls, stones or banks, or clothing more level areas in front of a border. The silvery evergreen foliage of this plant is of much greater value than the yellow flowers and can be used to create charming effects with other foliage of purplish hues or flowers of the deeper shades of blue, purple and crimson.

MORE EVERGREEN CARPETS

No plant excites my admiration more than one which will condescend to grow here, there and everywhere, maintain its composure whatever the hardships it is asked to endure or the indignities heaped upon it, still remain neat and tidy at all seasons and be extremely beautiful when it reaches its consummation. The dear old London pride, *Saxifraga × urbium*, better though incorrectly known as *S. umbrosa*, is such a plant. I know of no other plant which graces so uncomplainingly so many dingy little front gardens in the heart of towns and cities, is granted better living conditions in so many others; one which fits perfectly into the atmosphere of the old-world garden yet seldom looks out of place elsewhere.

Page 99 (above) Waldsteinia ternata for a low, shiny, evergreen carpet with yellow flowers in spring; *(below) Chamaepericlymenum canadense (Cornus canadensis).* A delightful ground coverer for acid soils

Page 100 (*above*) A mass of pink flowers in late summer, *Polygonum affine* later assumes rich autumn and winter foliage; (*below*) the non-flowering form of the lamb's-ears, *Stachys olympica* 'Silver Carpet', with silvery-grey woolly leaves

The London pride takes to all soils, even to those which are little more than stones and rubble. It endures the sun and revels in semi-shade, it gets trampled on and maligned, but it recovers and seldom fails to come up with its annual haze of pinkish-white flowers in the summer; and always its rosettes of leaves seem capable of merging into a complete, weed-repelling carpet. Lift the carpet, break it up into single rosettes each with a few roots, plant these again about 25cm (10in) apart each way and within a very short space of time the carpet is once again complete. This is how the plant should be used, not consigned, as so often, to those places where so many other plants will only languish and die. Its form, 'Aurea Punctata' ('Variegata Aurea'), whose leaves are blotched and mottled with yellow, is one of those plants which I dislike at close quarters but appreciate a little farther away. It really needs full sun to bring out its variegation.

Then there is its near cousin the foam flower, *Tiarella cordifolia*, which forms a 15cm (6in) high mat of evergreen leaves: these become richly burnished with bronze and reddish-pink shades from the first frosts until spring growth begins. With its questing, rooting, creeping stems it rapidly becomes a dense and spreading mass; it needs curbing slightly when it reaches the limit of its territory, but it cannot really be called invasive. It prefers some shade, so it is ideal for associating with shrubs; but it will not be deterred in full sun and this will probably lead to rather more intense coloration in the winter. Each year, in May and June, without fail it becomes a sheet of foamy white flowers from which it derives its common name. It is indeed one of the most thorough, dependable and beautiful of these short carpeting plants and a treasure in any garden.

I note that quite a few nurserymen now offer *Waldsteinia ternata*, so evidently its undoubted virtues as an evergreen ground coverer are at last being recognised. I love this plant because it thrives in the sticky clay soil of my garden, equally well where it is permanently moist or where it is made just as dry in summer through the avid surface roots of silver birches. It is just as much at home where the soil is light and well drained and cares not whether the situation is one of full sun or dense shade. Its foliage forms a 10cm (4in) high carpet of deep glossy green; it steadily thickens up and

G

spreads by means of short rooting runners, but it is never rampageous. Its yellow, strawberry-like flowers, although not freely produced, sit prettily on the foliage in early spring, with an occasional, localised second flowering a little later.

SWEET-SCENTED CARPETS

Everyone regards the lily-of-the-valley with a great deal of affection. It may be rather inclined perhaps to become starved in the centre of a colony, unless it is given a periodic top-dressing of humus – which is readily applied as it dies down annually – but it thrives in any type of soil, in sun or shade with, perhaps, a slight preference for some relief from scorching sun. There is no need for me to make further commendation, except to say that it should be planted more often for the purpose of clothing the ground and not be considered to have fulfilled its commitments when the last of its sweet flowers has faded.

I am amazed that our native sweet woodruff, *Galium* (*Asperula*) *odorata*, is not held in almost as much affection as the lily-of-the-valley. My memory goes back years to having seen great drifts of it in a wood: delicate-looking foliage bespangled with heads of white, starry, delightfully scented flowers in late spring, and a scent of new-mown hay when the leaves were cut and dried. For all its daintiness it is by no means so genteel in its habit for, given the chance, it can spread quite rapidly: it is best given quarters between shrubs or beneath trees – it loves shade – where it can do no harm when it sets off to wander.

ESPECIALLY FOR SHADY PLACES

For where the soil is acid and contains plenty of humus there are few finer carpeting plants than the partridge berry, *Gaultheria procumbens*, which extends steadily to form a dense, low, evergreen carpet speckled with tiny, white, bell-shaped flowers in late summer. These are succeeded by round scarlet fruits: the flowers and the fruits are often in evidence at the same time. The plant is also known as the creeping wintergreen, for its leaves when crushed emit the aroma of this well-known medicinal oil; and it is indeed one of the main sources of the oil. *Gaultheria* delights in shady conditions and is an ideal subject for grounding between rhododendrons, azaleas and similar shrubs requiring a lime-free soil.

The creeping dogwood, *Cornus canadensis*, now saddled with the rather inglorious change of name to *Chamaepericlymenum canadense* – which I am sure few people other than botanists will use – is also ideal for the same purpose and conditions. Though perhaps a trifle slow to get going, once it has become established it can start to travel by means of its underground shoots. It is no more than about 15 cm (6in) high. Its 'flowers' consist of four quite large white bracts surrounding the inconspicuous true flowers which are succeeded by a crop, usually rather sparse, of bright red fruits. The leaves assume rich, deep-red autumnal tints. While it can be used among suitable shrubs, nowhere does it look better than when carpeting moist ground beneath the shade of trees in a natural setting.

Although I had grown *Maianthemum bifolium* before, I had never really appreciated its carpeting capacity until I wandered through the moisture-laden woodlands near Kitsbuhel in the Tyrol. A rare native, it has broad, heart-shaped, glossy green leaves. In spring it thrusts up heads of little white, lily-of-the-valley-like flowers on short stems. It too likes shade, moisture and woodland soil.

So also does *Arisarum proboscideum*, which will form a mat of deep green, shiny, spear-shaped leaves. Under the leaves are little brown and white flowers which are really arum-like spathes with long 'tails' surrounding the true flowers, looking like little mice lurking in the shadows. I have found that *Arisarum*, while it likes moisture, will also quite happily clothe the ground where summer drought and trees prevail, provided it is not exposed to the sun. Unfortunately, it tends to die down in late summer, but by that time it will have done its job of helping to keep weeds at bay.

RATHER MORE VIGOROUS GROWERS

Polygonum is a genus of variable character. Some of its members are tantalising weeds; others are giant invasive perennials, handsome in their own right but not plants for the smaller garden. There are the well-known Russian vine, *P. baldshuanicum*, a climber which needs considerable space, and more elite carpeting species like *P. affine* and *P. vaccinifolium*. The first named is a controllable spreader, forming a dense low mat of narrow, bright green leaves which turn to rich shades of russet-red then brown for the winter. Its short spikes of pink flowers are not produced until late summer, and they are particularly valuable at that season. It has two good forms: 'Darjeeling Red' with rosy-crimson flowers; and 'Donald Lowndes' ('Lowndes Variety'), rather more compact in habit, with rose flowers fading to deep red. One has to watch these polygonums, for after a year or two there is a tendency for them to die off in the crown if the soil becomes impoverished: then is the time to start thinking about lifting, dividing and replanting them after fortifying the soil.

P. vaccinifolium is rather different in habit. It sends out over the surface long thin shoots which root freely and soon set up a matted canopy over the ground. It is especially good for covering a slope where there is the odd large stone for it to cascade over; and it delights the eye with its abundant display of long-lasting short spikes of pink flowers in late summer and early autumn – a real last fling to the summer.

Setting kin against kin is not often practised in gardening. On seeing *Lamium maculatum* used as ground cover, more than one person has commented to me, 'What! Dead-nettles!' There the similarity ends, for this is a perfectly good weed-suppressor growing around 15 cm (6 in) high, linking up with prostrate growths which will root where they touch the ground and forming a nice evergreen coverage of greyish-green rounded leaves, each with a broad, silvery, central band. The purplish-pink flowers are very reminiscent of the weed species and are of a difficult, hard colour which does not readily associate with others. Those who have aversions to it can turn to the pink form, 'Roseum', or to the very pleasant white 'Album'. There is also a golden-leaved form, 'Aureum', which is somewhat slower in growth, rather less accommodating and inclined to scorch in hot sun. Propagation of any of these is simplicity in itself, for all the forms will root in a few days from cuttings; and self-sown seedlings are usually available, although these are likely to be the purplish type, whatever the colour of the parent plants.

Creeping Jenny will be familiar to most home gardeners. Rather a rampant little plant, *Lysimachia nummularia* should never be placed where its habit of spreading by rooting stems cannot be contained. It is ideal for wandering through shrub-beds, and it will stud itself with golden flowers in summer. Its golden-leaved form, 'Aurea', is rather more reserved and less inclined to make a nuisance of itself; it does best in partial shade.

OF POTENTILLA AND OTHERS

The worth of the shrubby potentillas has been discussed earlier on this book and here we look at another plant from this genus, the prostrate *P. alba*, which spreads out its growths to form mats 30cm (12in) across. It has greyish-green, silvery-edged leaves and, like its shrubby relatives, is seldom without a few of its white, orange-centred flowers throughout the summer months following the main display in late spring. If one can obtain it, *P. cuneata* is another good, low coverer with small, deep green, trifoliate leaves and yellow flowers in midsummer.

The lamb's-tongue plant, *Stachys olympica* (*S. lanata*), is making a name for itself as a ground coverer: it forms a dense low mat of large, silvery-grey, woolly leaves. The majority of these leaves die off in winter, so the plant needs to be cleaned out in spring before growth starts again, and at the same time a little top-dressing should be worked in to prevent the appearance of bare patches. The mauve flowers on 45cm (18in) high stems are rather irregularly produced, are of no great value and do tend to detract from the foliage. It is better to grow the non-flowering form called 'Silver Carpet'. This is essentially a plant for the sun and a well-drained soil, although it does condescend to flourish in partial shade better than one might suppose, provided there is not too much winter damp round the crowns.

Blue-eyed Mary, *Omphalodes verna*, and *O. cappadocica* have sky-blue flowers. The former is the shorter of the two, a mere 10cm (4in) high. It starts producing its little white-throated bright blue, forget-me-not-like flowers as early as March. It has a very pretty white-flowered form called 'Alba'. *O. cappadocica* is about twice the height of *O. verna* and its flowers, of a deeper shade and wholly blue, follow a little later in the spring. It is rather more tufted in habit and retains its leaves for much of the winter. Both produce delightful spring flowers, and are ideal as base coats for the taller *Narcissus* species and hybrids referred to at the beginning of this chapter. *O. cappadocica* also associates well with the yellow bracts of *Euphorbia epithymoides* (*E. polychroma*), itself a useful, spreading herbaceous plant. Both of the omphalodes fill in well with rooting stems, and they have a liking for partial shade.

The native self-heal, *Prunella vulgaris*, is no mean flowering plant but, as we have noted previously, it can become a persistent lawn weed. It has relatives which can be employed as opposition to weeds: *P. webbiana* is a more than useful carpet-rooting plant, making a low mat of foliage from which spring 30cm (12in) high stems bearing rosy-purple flowers quite late in the summer. There are variations, of which 'Alba', with white flowers, is the most pronounced; partial shade and a reasonably moist soil will satisfy its modest requirements.

I suppose we could term the accepted garden forms of violas and pansies as ground-covering plants, but here I want to end with a lesser-known little violet, *Viola labradorica*. This has leaves fully permeated with purplish-maroon, especially when young, and with lavender flowers which, unfortunately, like so many of those of the *Viola* species, are quite devoid of scent. Although it will grow well in shade, its foliage hue is more intense in full sun. It roots laterally, to form a close colony, assisted by self-sown seedlings which are apt to spring up some distance away. These seedlings do not usually make a nuisance of themselves, for they are not difficult to eradicate if unwanted.

Ground-cover plants should never be regarded as mere assistants in the garden. Apart from the virtues they themselves may possess – and some of these are quite considerable – they can usually be employed to enhance the appearance and the value of other plants which may tower above them.

CHAPTER TWELVE

BLANKETS FOR DWARF BULBS

Still concerned with carpeting or mat-forming plants, we now move right down the scale to those which are only a few centimetres high. Naturally, the dwarfer a plant the less impenetrable it becomes, and one must be honest and admit that such lowly plants are by no means weed-smotherers. But they do clothe the ground, and they either prevent the successful germination of weed seeds or effectively choke most of the young seedlings, depending on the type. They cannot be expected to do this to the stronger thrusting weeds or those which infiltrate insidiously. Neither can they counter completely the prolific seeders like annual meadow-grass, which will germinate virtually on a grain of soil provided there is moisture, and if allowed to seed profusely in the near vicinity may well get a foothold among these carpeting plants. But one cannot have a big strong army everywhere, and even if one has occasionally to assist these little defenders by pulling out trespassers and periodically replanting, they will still do a good job of carpeting the ground.

Everyone loves the dwarf spring bulbs: the snowdrops, crocuses, scillas, chionodoxas, miniature daffodils, dogstooth-violets and the like. Yet, all too often people do not provide sufficient ground coverage upon which the bulbs can display their charms. And, more important, ground coverage gives summer furnishing to the earth, thus preventing damage to the bulbs when they have died down and all too often are forgotten for a spell. This coverage must be either such that makes most of its growth after the bulbous subjects have faded away or such that they can readily thrust up through it. Obviously, therefore, a perennial carpet is the answer, a base coat which can be used effectively to show off the flowers of early spring.

Almost without exception the plants which follow spread and root as they go; and once a few plants have developed into a patch it is comparatively easy to lift them, split them into numerous small pieces and have enough to cover a much greater area. It is essential that the gaps should be closed as speedily as possible after planting, for if weeds get a hold first and are not thoroughly eradicated, they will probably prove too great an obstacle for the carpeting plants. In all cases, therefore, planting around 15–25cm (6–10in) apart should be the maximum. If the number required is too expensive, it is much better to be content with planting a small area, using this as a stock ground for future extension in the manner described above.

GREEN BLANKETS

Pictures of a chamomile lawn spring to mind. Frankly, I consider this to be more of a pipe-dream than a ready alternative to a grass lawn, for as such it is not without its problems. But the common chamomile, *Chamaemelum nobile* (*Anthemis nobilis*), especially the non-flowering dwarf form 'Treneague', when used in a more confined space, can be an excellent green base for the smaller bulbs. Further to that, of course, there is the rather pungent aroma given off when the leaves are brushed against or trodden on which compensates for the comparative insignificance or absence of flowers.

I have often thought that *Cotula squalida* might have possibilities for lawn-making because it will infiltrate into turf and stand mowing, but it is inclined to be wiry in the stem and it does go brown and die down during the winter. But again, in the right place – and this must be one where it can either be confined or has tolerant neighbours – it will serve a similar purpose to chamomile. It has bright green, feathery leaves which turn an attractive bronze as they age and small, rather insignificant yellow flowers.

There may be nothing very exciting about the rupture wort, *Herniaria glabra*, but its very low mat consisting of thin prostrate stems clothed with shining dark green leaves makes it a first-class unobtrusive base plant at all seasons for any corner or small area

BLANKETS FOR DWARF BULBS 109

where dwarf spring bulbs are the main feature. While the rupture wort may be so controllable that it can be introduced into a rock-garden, *Helxine soleirolii*, the plant that is popularly grown in pots and under greenhouse stages, wending its way up moist green-house walls when it really gets going and universally called 'mind your own business', certainly has earned its nickname. It can be almost as rampant and invasive in the open, especially in a moist and shady position, although it is subject to frost damage. While it will make an excellent, low, bright evergreen carpet, it should be introduced only where it is not going to become a weed. It has both golden and silvery counterparts which may be slightly less vigorous and very much inclined to revert to green; nevertheless, the pattern of gold and silver with green in such a carpet can be quite appealing.

Two forms of sandwort, *Arenaria balearica* and *A. montana*, both make flat green blankets which become studded with little white flowers in profusion in early summer. The former is little more than 12mm (½in) high, likes shade and is sufficiently restricted to use in a rock-garden. *A. montana*, with growth 7·5cm (3in) high, likes full sun and is not so ready to stay at home; but it can be a picture when it is sprawling over a bank, flowing over a wall or is used as groundwork among dwarf frontal shrubs.

Hydrocotyle moschata is not well known, but it is offered as a good ground-covering and paving plant by several nurserymen. Its flowers are of no account but it has nice round, glossy green leaves and grows in sun or shade.

SILVER, GOLD AND VARIEGATED BLANKETS

For solid silver all-year-round encrustation over the ground there is nothing to beat mountain everlasting, *Antennaria dioica*. Its growth consists of small rosettes of closely packed silver-grey leaves rising no more than 2·5cm (1in) above ground level, most of these rooting at the base and forming a ready means of propagation when a mat is lifted and the rosettes are dibbled in 10–15cm (4–6in) apart to start a fresh colony. Although it is supposed to be a plant for the sun and for light well-drained soil, I have found that it takes to most conditions, even clay and shade; and while it may be classed primarily as a carpeting plant for a rock-garden or bank, I have used it in all sorts of places as a blanket for bulbs. As such it is an ideal base for purple crocuses and for the blue flowers of squills, chionodoxas and the like. It produces an 'everlasting' type of white flower, pinkish in the form 'Rosea', on 25cm (10in) stems. The flowers are pretty in their own way, but I remove them as soon as I have cut sufficient for drying, to expose the silver carpet which I value most.

On page 27 you will find reference to the pearlwort, *Sagina procumbens*, one of the most persistent and difficult lawn weeds, but the same cannot be said of its golden relation, *S. glabra* 'Aurea', for although this can quickly form large golden mats, it does tend to die out in patches and needs periodic replanting. This may reduce its value as a stifler of weeds, but even this chore of replanting can be a worthwhile alternative to constant weeding.

In nature *Glechoma hederacea* (*Nepeta glechoma*) carpets woodlands and is commonly known as ground ivy, although it bears little resemblance to and has no relationship to ivy proper. I am rather fond of the silver-variegated form 'Variegata', which is often grown as a trailing plant in pots, for it starts off the season with the young growing tips delicately stained with pink, and as these lengthen and begin to trail, the whole becomes a sheet of greyish-green leaves liberally banded with silvery white. It likes to wander and should therefore be confined to ground covering among shrubs, or be given room to deploy itself on a bank or in woodland.

The silver-variegated bugle, *Ajuga reptans* 'Variegata', is much easier to keep confined. Unlike its richly maroon-foliaged relatives, it is rather happier in places where it escapes the midday sun. It is really charming when it produces its clear blue flowers on short stems furnished with small variegated leaves, some of them almost completely white.

AJUGAS AND ACAENAS

Continuing with the bugles we come to *Ajuga reptans* 'Atropurpureum', with purple-maroon foliage and bluish-purple flowers. This is ideal for fronting and grounding out silver-foliaged shrubs and plants and in combination with other flowers. Or one can employ a slight variation in *A. r.* 'Multicolor' ('Rainbow'), whose deeply coloured leaves are spotted and splashed with green, yellow, red and bronze. In direct contrast, *A. r.* 'Alba' has green foliage and white flowers.

Although these ajugas do not die off completely, the dark-foliaged ones in particular do lose quite a lot of their leaves, but there are usually enough left to form a very effective groundwork for spring bulbs. It is an easy matter to keep patches nourished by working in a spring top-dressing, and if replanting becomes necessary or if one wants to increase the planting, propagation is simplicity in itself. When the plants are passing out of flower, short procumbent stems called stolons push out, each producing a tuft of leaves which roots where it touches the ground. Curtail-ment of patches is easy: it is a matter only of cutting off the outside stolons, or allowing them to root and then using the young plants for planting elsewhere.

The acaenas or New Zealand burrs produce creeping, rooting stems and quickly form dense low mats. They are not plants for the rock-garden for they can take some dislodging when they wander between stones and other plants, but with space to spread they will make marvellous evergreen carpets through which very few weeds attempt to push. There is *Acaena microphylla* with bronzy-green leaves, *A. buchananii* of metallic pea-green tone, and the rather taller and stronger *A.* 'Blue Haze' with really attractive blue-green foliage. All have inconspicuous flowers, but *A. microphylla* does follow with heads or burrs of quite bright red, spiny fruits. All are good also as paving plants, for they are tough and wiry and will stand quite a lot of rough treatment in the way of misplaced feet.

THE THYMES

Perhaps of all low, green carpeting plants the thymes have most to commend them. By far the commonest, *Thymus drucei* (*T. serpyllum* of gardens) which inhabits rocky banks, cliffs and moorlands and filters into the close turf to regale the eyes with a sheet of rosy-purple flowers and to titillate the nostrils when trodden or sat upon, is a charming plant for the rock-garden and for carpeting between or in front of the more upright growing heaths or other plants. Its spread is controllable and although it does produce seedlings around, these need cause no concern. There are garden forms with flowers of red, white or various shades of pink; and a mixed mat can be a delightful patchwork of colour. As a variation one can also grow *T. hirsutus doefleri* and *T. lanuginosus*, both with grey-green foliage and lilac-pink flowers.

SEDUMS AND OTHERS

While I would not regard the stonecrops as ideal weed-quellers, there are several which make very good, effective carpets, avoiding like the plague *Sedum acre* and *S. anglicum*, denounced previously. *S. spurium* is one of the most vigorous spreaders; the type has pink flowers and its form 'Schorbusser Blut' deep red, while 'Green Mantle' is virtually non-flowering and is the best coverer of all. My favourites are two forms of *S. spathulifolium*: 'Purpureum', whose leaves are at first coated with white farina which imparts a silver sheen and then, as summer comes to an end, turn to a deep, mealy purple; and the rather dwarfer 'Capa Blanca' which does not undergo this change. Both forms have yellow flowers, tend to be carpet-rooting in a limited way and need planting fairly close together, about 20cm (8in), to get good coverage. Increase is easy, for the plants will divide readily and as with the invasive stonecrops, little bits broken off and left on the ground invariably take root; but one need have no fears that this propensity will make them the insidious invaders that the common stonecrops are.

There are other sedums, like *S. album* 'Murale' with bronzy foliage, which are all worth trying in suitable situations where there is full sun and the soil is sound and well drained. Ideally they should be placed in those parts of a rock-garden or rocky bank where these conditions appertain, but there are often little 'pockets' adjacent to paths where they can do a good job also.

The blue shamrock, *Parochetus communis*, is a plant worth searching for if one is wanting 'something rather different'. Given a position with partial shade and shelter it can be quite vigorous, forming close mats of clover-like foliage, each leaflet fascinatingly

marked with a zigzag purplish-brown line. For this foliage alone
it is well worth having. It also produces delightful, pea-like,
gentian-blue flowers during the winter months, although their
appearance and beauty may be dependent on spells of mild
weather. The whole plant may even suffer in a severe winter, so it
is really only a subject for the more congenial places.

The sea heath, *Frankenia thymifolia*, also warrants consideration.
Its absolutely flat mats of grey-green foliage are studded throughout the summer with tiny pink flowers. As its common name
implies, this is a subject which does exceptionally well in coastal
areas, in light soil and full sun.

Reiterating what I said at the beginning of this chapter, one must
not regard these very dwarf carpeting plants as inviolate to weeds;
but once they have linked up – provided they have not been
planted in soil abounding with perennial weeds or weed seeds
generally, and that none of these are allowed to become established while there is still bare soil between the ground cover –
they will make an area far less receptive to weed growth and be
an asset to the garden visually, with or without suitable bulbous
companions.

CHAPTER THIRTEEN

CLUMP-FORMING GROUND COVERERS

A wide range of plants, by virtue of their basal hummocks and their ability to go on from year to year growing steadily larger to form dense colonies and doing this without requiring regular attention in the way of lifting, dividing and replanting, can be employed to combat weeds in those parts of a garden where permanent planting is required.

This group does perhaps need just a little more annual attention that those plants whose creeping stems above and below ground eventually envelop the whole surface with top growth. They all have flowering qualities to vie with their foliage: in several cases the flowering stems temporarily increase their overall height to twice or more that of the foliage alone, and this means that one must have a mind to the plants' immediate associates, especially those behind. Some are quite suitable for the forefront of the herbaceous border; however, the natural parts of the garden are more in keeping. Generally they are fine for associating with shrubs either as frontal subjects to a bed or border, or in a more natural setting where their less formal habit and generally undemanding nature are far more appropriate than those of many of the popular herbaceous perennials.

With some it is necessary to remove the flowering stems when spent so that they do not detract from the main asset, the foliage. This is not usually a very laborious chore. The deciduous ones may have to be trimmed or cleaned over after they have died down; a job I like to do after the worst of the winter is over, and not immediately leaf-fall has ceased. Indeed, I have no 'winter-tidy' mind for I find that even dead foliage, provided it has not reached a disreputable state, is better than the bareness of prim tidiness. It is a lingering reminder of summer and, perhaps more important, it is nature's winter protection to dormant crowns and roots.

In most cases it is easy to put on a spring mulch between the clumps, and when I do this I do not remove fallen tree-leaves unless they are in excess or liable to move and make other parts of the garden untidy. I place my compost mulch on these leaves, pinning them down and capping the surface against the germination of seedling weeds. I know that my compost is unlikely to be weed-seed free, for it contains grass mowings, and these are invariably a source of infestation by annual meadow-grass. The roots of germinating weeds do however find some difficulty in penetrating the underlying leaf layer; and any drying out of the mulch and the spring growth of the ground cover generally quickly spell doom to these weed seedlings.

A broad guide to planting distances has been given in the introductory chapter; if there is any departure from the 30–45cm (12–18in) average it will be given when I discuss any subject which requires rather more or less space.

EVERGREEN HUMMOCKS

Naturally, these must be accounted the most valuable, for such plants give all-year-round coverage. Possibly the densest and most effective is *Galax aphylla* with tough-looking, rounded, glossy, deep green foliage which becomes attractively burnished with reddish-bronze in winter. In June the 45cm (18in) long flower stems produce tapering, erect spikes of white flowers to brighten up the shady places which this plant loves – and it will grow in quite dense shade. Its only other requisite is a lime-free soil containing plenty of humus.

Becoming deservedly popular, especially with the flower arranger, the false alum root, *Tellima grandiflora* also puts on a winter foliage coat, the bright green of its summer one changing gradually to a rich, deep red as winter gets under way. The leaves have fairly long stems and make excellent material for a winter floral arrangement; the exponent of this art also delights in the 60–75cm (24–30in) stems which carry creamy-white flowers in midsummer. The removal of these when spent is about the only service one has to give to the plant.

The closely related alum root, *Heuchera*, is rather similar in habit and foliage, although without the winter change of coat. It is prized for its long thin stems of feathery panicles of tiny flowers. Most of the garden cultivars are forms or hybrids of *H. sanguinea* and include such good kinds as 'Red Spangles', 'Scintillation' (with pink, red-tipped flowers) and 'Pearl Drops' (pinkish-white), together with excellent mixed strains. *Heuchera* was hybridised with its cousin the foam flower, *Tiarella cordifolia*, whose virtues I have previously extolled, and produced the bigeneric hybrid × *Heucherella tiarelloides*, generally somewhat shorter in the flower stem and most profuse with its haze of pink flowers in late spring and early summer.

Phlomis russelliana (*P. viscosa* of gardens) is a plant of considerable character, both in foliage and flower. In June, from the great, gradually spreading clump of large, crinkled, hairy, sage-green leaves appear strong, square flower stems up to 90cm (36in) high, bearing smaller leaves and successive dense whorls of hooded flowers, as many as fifty per whorl, each with fawn-yellow hoods and soft yellow lips, a quiet but fascinating combination of colour in unusual array. A group needs a natural background; an isolated plant elsewhere can be a focal point. It produces numerous self-sown seedlings which can be easily transplanted or just as easily destroyed. Sun and a well-drained soil are what this plant ought to have, but I have also given it semi-shade and a wet foothold and it has not complained.

Two hybrid comfreys, *Symphytum* 'Hidcote Pink' and 'Hidcote Blue', both arising probably from the colonising dwarf Russian comfrey, *S. grandiflorum*, are sufficiently evergreen to be included here. Both, at about 45cm (18in) high, are rather taller than *grandiflorum* and do not have its capacity to send out prostrate shoots. They have the same large, hoary, deep green leaves and bear pink and blue (pink-tipped in bud) flowers respectively. They too thrive in moist shady conditions, making them ideal filler plants among or fronting shrubs, or clothing the shady banks of a stream.

Page 117 (*above*) The starry white flowers of *Arenaria balearica* appear to twinkle over its flat green carpet of foliage; (*below*) the mealy white of the summer foliage of *Sedum spathulifolium* 'Purpureum' turns to deep mealy purple in autumn

Page *118* (*above*) *Hosta crispula*, one of the many useful and effective plantain lilies; (*below*) The spotted leaves of *Pulmonaria officinalis* lend accent to a shady spot in the author's garden

Like periwinkles and rose of Sharon for colonising, the plantain lilies have achieved a lot of repute for ground cover in a different way. They are essentially plants for partial or even full shade, though they will not object to full sun if there is adequate moisture underfoot. They are plants of architectural bearing; the leaves have form and texture and variations of tone, and the upright stems of pendent flowers, mostly of pale lilac, are always pleasing. They will go on and on for years without replanting provided they are given a periodic top-dressing; they transplant with ease and can be chopped up into pieces to increase stock. They may be used in the forefront of the herbaceous border, but this is not really their home; as fillers in front of shrubs or associated with water, they look much more in keeping.

There are numerous species and cultivars to choose from. For rich green one can select the fairly robust *Hosta ventricosa*, *H. undulata* 'Erromena' or *H.* 'Honeybells' of slightly paler hue and with scented flowers, down to the 30cm (12in) high *H. lancifolia*. Of those with glaucous bluish-green leaves, *H. sieboldiana elegans* and *H. fortunei hyacinthina* make splendid specimen plants 60cm (24in) or more high and as much across. I prefer to see these planted no more than a maximum of three together, otherwise some of their noble character is lost. *H. fortunei* itself is of average height and is slightly glaucous blue-green.

Starting off the season, *H. fortunei* 'Albopicta' is at first bright yellow, edged with green and *H.f.* 'Aurea' is wholly yellow; then they begin to change gradually until by about midsummer they become wholly green.

A number of variegated hostas give welcome, tasteful and not discordant variation to the foliage tones. *H. albomarginata*, *H.* 'Thomas Hogg', *H. fortunei* 'Marginata Alba' and *H. crispula*, the latter with wavy margins to its leaves, are all edged with creamy white and *H. ventricosa* 'Variegata' with creamy yellow. In contrast, this colour variation is a broad, creamy central band with *H. ventricosa* 'Aureomaculata' and *H.* undulata, the latter with attractively waved leaf margins.

H

This is only a selection of the hostas which are readily available to give character to the garden, to furnish shady parts and to smother weeds effectively. That they die down completely in winter does not reduce their value for the last-named purpose.

MORE HARDY GERANIUMS

Here again there is a quite large number from which to make a selection, so I shall mention a few of those I know best as being among the most suitable in habit for short to medium ground cover. *Geranium macrorrhizum* has already had its praises sung on page 92. Another favourite of mine is *G. renardii* with soothing, reticulated, velvety, grey-green foliage which forms an ideal base for the white flowers which are delicately veined with purplish-mauve. *G. endressii* has rose-pink flowers and is in bloom for much of the summer; there are slight variations of floral tone in its cultivars, 'Wargrave Pink' and 'Rose Clair'. Among the more vigorous spreaders, *G.* 'Claridge Druce' with magenta-pink flowers and *G. sanguineum* 'Glenluce' of a softer shade of pink, are splendid for the purpose.

A change of floral tone is provded by *G.* 'Johnson's Blue', or *G. wallichianum* 'Buxton's Blue', of more trailing habit and particularly effective where a low formation is required. Although they will not produce any great splash of colour, there is something strangely compelling in the dusky purplish-black flowers of the mourning widow, *G. phaeum*; this plant has first-class dark green foliage and a capacity to flourish in the dry shade of large trees.

Generally, these geraniums give of their best in partial shade, and although they die down or lose their foliage completely during the winter and may need a little tidying up when spring comes round once more, they will do a splendid job, often in situations where some plants may be unhappy, and they always look more at home when their surroundings are not too formal.

LUNGWORTS AND MASTERWORTS

According to my dictionary the suffix of wort means any herb or vegetable, so it is not surprising that it is quite commonly used in connection with the common names of plants. In the case of lung-wort, *Pulmonaria*, it would appear that this originated from the spotted leaves of *P. officinalis* being likened to diseased lungs. Both this species and the Bethlehem sage, *P. picta* (*P. saccharata*), make splendid broad masses of large, hoary, deep green leaves liberally spotted with white. These spring up after a display of pink flowers which turn to blue, combining colours which are especially welcome when the plants flower from late February onwards.

P. rubra, with green leaves, has soft red flowers in evidence at the same time, while *P. angustifolia*, also with green leaves, blooms a little later and is a delightful shade of clear bright blue, especially fine in the forms 'Munstead Variety' and 'Mawson's Variety'.

These pulmonarias do need plenty of moisture at the roots as well as partial shade, especially from the midday sun which will often cause them to flag. While they will go on for years I am disposed to lift, split and replant them occasionally to keep them in full vigour. At about 30cm (12in) or a little more apart, they soon link up again.

Masterwort I cannot define. The name has been applied to several plants, but here I use it in conjunction with the astrantias, a genus which produces long-lasting flowers of the papery 'everlasting' type, quiet in coloration but extremely charming and desirable for cutting. *Astrantia major*, with whitish flowers on stems around 60cm (24in) high above its basal clump of leaves, is probably the most vigorous clother; it has an extremely good cream-and-yellow variegated form in 'Sunningdale Variegated'. I would also add *A. carniolica* 'Rosea' and *A.c.* 'Rubra' to my collection, for the greater beauty and usefulness of their pink and deep red flowers. Remember that here there will be spent flower stems to remove if they have not already gone as cut flowers, and it is well to do this as soon as the last flowers fade for these plants tend to be quite prolific self-seeders.

PRIMULAS AS GROUND COVER

In my opinion the hardy primulas are not exploited enough for this purpose. I started using them when I was employing the drumstick primula, *Primula denticulata*, for spring bedding in public parks. Finding it much more convenient to raise new stock annually from seeds, each year I had thousands of splendid plants being consigned to the rubbish heap after they had completed their stint in the beds; so I started planting some of them between shrubs, primarily to give added spring colour. After flowering this primula makes colossal growth and keeps most weeds in subjection very effectively.

There are other species, mainly in the candelabra section, like *P. japonica*, *P. pulverulenta*, *P. beesiana* and *P. burmanica* which likewise produce very strong tufts of leaves after flowering, and I need hardly add that with these one can have ground cover par excellence combined with a colourful and long-lasting display of flowers.

Most primulas must be assured of adequate moisture at the roots during the summer, otherwise they will languish; and while many show a preference for a soil with plenty of humus in it, the strong-growing ones I have mentioned are by no means choosey. Indeed in my own garden I dug holes in the solid yellow clay of a weed-ridden bank and literally shoved in some one-year-old plants of *P. denticulata*, giving each no more than a handful of soil to cover the roots: all have thrived and have more than held their own with the weeds.

LADY'S-MANTLE AND OTHERS

What a splendid name lady's-mantle is for *Alchemilla mollis*, so aptly describing its foamy masses of soft, sulphury-yellow flowers in midsummer. But there is more than a challenge to floral beauty in the large, beautifully rounded, lobed, grey-green leaves so velvety to the touch and so full of texture and character, doing a more humble job in an aristocratic way. Give the plants about 45cm (18in) space in sun or shade, trim them up each spring and with a little top-dressing at the same time they will be happy for several years, a ready source of cut foliage and flower throughout the summer. The many self-sown seedlings liable to spring up should not really become a nuisance.

For permanency there are few plants to equal barrenworts, *Epimedium*. They may not be quick to establish themselves and fill in, so generally speaking 30cm (12in) apart is about the distance to plant them; but they do extend steadily and will fill in eventually with a tidy mat of growth about the same measurement in height. Their delightful little spurred, columbine-like flowers are produced in spring, but with most species they are inclined to be rather short-stemmed and hidden away among the old growths. It therefore pays to treat these subjects like *Hypericum calycinum* and to shear them down just before growth begins, to expose the flowers and also to encourage new growth which, with *E.* × *versicolor* and its variant 'Sulphureum' and *E.* × *rubrum* in particular, carries light green, unfurling leaves which are delicately burnished with bronze when young. These have yellow, primrose and red flowers respectively.

E. perralderanum with yellow flowers is probably the best ground coverer; or one can turn to *E. pinnatum* 'Colchicum', another yellow, or to *E.* × *warleyense* with attractive coppery orange flowers, and to several others. The latter, with *E.* × *versicolor* and its variant, are again quite colourful throughout the winter, when their foliage becomes burnished with bronze and copper. *E.* × *youngianum* 'Niveum', with bronzed young leaves and pure white flowers, is one of the daintiest forms of the genus and makes very good ground cover where a degree of refinement is required. All delight in cool, shady conditions and reasonably good soil.

So closely allied that anyone can be forgiven for mistaking it for an epimedium, *Vancouveria hexandra* is an even lighter edition with dainty, pleasant green foliage above which the small white flowers in upright panicles protrude in May and June. It likes the same conditions as do the epimediums.

My favourite *Dicentra* is the old bleeding heart, *D. spectabilis*. Although they may not be particularly dense with their 30cm (12in) high finely cut foliage, *D. formosa* 'Bountiful' and the rather stronger *D. eximia* 'Adrian Bloom' are well worth growing for this foliage alone. Their long-displayed flowers, with 'Bountiful' in particular, undergo a gradual, hardly noticeable transition to somewhat duller but almost as attractive seed-vessels. The white *D. eximia* 'Alba' is another good form, with rather more green leaves, and it is extremely profuse in flower.

The sky-blue, forget-me-not-like flowers of *Brunnera macro-phylla* (*Anchusa myosotidiflora*), thrusting up in sprays from the large, hoary, light green 45cm (18in) foliage, last throughout May and most of June, and there is often a partial secondary display a little later. It looks fine with a backing of the yellow flowers of doronicums or against golden-toned or silver-toned shrubs, and it is best in moist soil in partial shade. As it tends to push out a few short underground stems for extension purposes it can be planted 60cm (24in) apart. Look out also for the variegated form 'Variegata', whose leaves are broadly and tastefully edged with cream. Although it colours best in full sun where it makes good clump-forming ground cover, the golden marjoram, *Origanum vulgare* 'Aureum', can be associated with the *Brunnera* in partial shade to form a pretty combination of blue flowers fringed with golden foliage in spring. As summer advances, the foliage of the marjoram tends to lose some of its intense gold but the plant remains bright and cheerful.

Lastly, a plant so well-known that it needs no description, is the ever-popular catmint, *Nepeta* × *faassenii* (*N. mussinii* of gardens) and the more vigorous garden form named 'Six Hills Giant'. They never seem to be misplaced whether they are used as herbaceous plants in the border, for fronting shrubs, spreading over the top of a stone retaining wall or as a group in a rock-garden – provided this is a fairly large one. Aromatic grey-green foliage and lavender-blue flowers throughout the summer make them as valuable as they are carefree, and I need say no more except to advise against complete annual trimming back before winter's blasts are over.

CHAPTER FOURTEEN

RAMPANT GROUND COVERERS

It may be that only those with fairly large gardens will have the space to introduce rampant plants with impunity. Occasionally however, in a quite small garden there is a problem place to clothe, and in any event this chapter will serve as a warning to those with no room for space-consuming plants, for several of those that I shall mention are offered quite freely as ground cover, or just as garden plants, without any real indication of their powers to take possession.

As they are rapid growers or intrepid spreaders there is no need to plant them closely to obtain quick and adequate coverage, but spacing must be governed by how much they will be expected to fend for themselves, to fight and win a running battle with weeds and to overcome the great majority with the minimum of assistance. Most of these plants root as they go and so their ultimate spread is indefinite. By comparison with all those which have been described earlier and which are either confined or readily confinable, far fewer plants will be required to cover a given area adequately; we need not therefore bother to even attempt to estimate their ultimate spread but should plant them distances apart which provide for a link-up in reasonable time so that they can present a united front. Assuming that there will be a fair amount of early competition, the distances apart which I shall suggest will be based on this reasoning.

THE IVIES

One accepts that these are more controllable than most plants in this group; and they are indeed employed in more hallowed parts than rough banks and difficult places. I could have included some of the less vigorous, small-leaved kinds in one of the preceding chapters; but even these have powers to go on and on and ivies generally, although they do not actually poison the ground as is sometimes supposed, do seem to make it untenable for most non-woody plants. They are extremely useful for carpeting beneath trees, for they are lovers of shade and will thrive where it is most dense. So also do certain weeds and less delectable native plants like dog's-mercury, and these may need suppressing but with the minimum of effort.

Common ivy, *Hedera helix*, is too ubiquitous and too prone to climb up trees and shrubs to be used except in the really unimportant places where there is plenty of room and where there are no trees and shrubs of consequence. The Irish ivy, *H.h.* 'Hibernica', is much better if a green mantle is required, for it is less inclined to climb.

Today, thanks to the vogue in house plants, forms of ivy are almost legion, and many of those which are now so commonly used as trained pot plants are perfectly hardy and well adapted for a ground-cover role in the open. The large-leaved, silver-variegated *H. canariensis* 'Variegata' ('Gloire de Marengo'), is ideal, although it may 'scorch' a little in severe weather. So too is the golden-variegated *H. colchica* 'Dentata Variegata', with even larger leaves, while of the small-leaved types I have found the silver-variegated *H. helix* 'Glacier' and the green *H.h.* 'Gold-heart', with golden centres to its leaves, exceptionally good; and there are many others. Whenever a pot plant of ivy, whatever the variety, becomes too large, it is a simple matter to root a few cuttings for replacement and transfer the old plant outside on trial as ground cover if a suitable position is available.

As for distances apart, I suggest thinking in terms of around 1·5m (5ft) each way for the common and Irish ivies and the other large-leaved forms, scaling this down to around 90cm (36in) for the small-leaved kinds, in order to obtain reasonably quick, close coverage. If there is no hurry to get the final results, these distances can be increased.

OTHER CLIMBERS AS GROUND COVER

One has only to see the traveller's-joy of the hedgerows, *Clematis vitalba*, in the limestone districts where it flourishes best, festooning a bank as well as climbing trees and hedges and completely obliterating all soft weeds, to appreciate that climbing plants may be made to serve two functions. I do not suggest that one should plant this extremely rampant native plant although it is not without considerable charm, particularly during the winter with its silvery haze of seed-heads. Why not turn, however, to that other very vigorous, popular and exceedingly beautiful species, *C. montana* which, although it displays its profusion of early flowers best when growing upright, so often has to be curtailed when on a wall or fence otherwise it will become an embarrassment.

The evergreen honeysuckle, *Lonicera japonica* 'Halliana', also soon becomes a tangled uncontrollable mass when its support is restricted, and like most honeysuckles it really requires the freedom of trees and bushes to scramble over. Let it crawl on the ground and its vigour may well be increased, for its stems will then root and spread the load of obtaining nutrition; and there is no reason why other vigorous honeysuckles like *L. americana* should not be tried for the purpose. After all, they can be raised very readily from cuttings and one plant will cover a lot of space.

Those autumn spectaculars, the self-clinging Virginia creepers, will also prostrate themselves and cascade down banks. The true Virginia creeper, *Parthenocissus* (*Vitis*) *quinquefolia*, with deeply cut palmate leaves, is to be preferred to the Boston ivy, *P. tricuspidata* (*Vitis inconstans*), with lobed leaves; which is the better of the two for growing on a wall. Then there is the magnificent ornamental vine, *Vitis coignetiae*, with leaves up to 30cm (12in) across, ablaze in shades of scarlet and deep crimson in the autumn. This too is a rampant grower, with more than a fifty-fifty chance of securing domination when given a subservient role.

Another climber requiring far more space aloft than many small gardens can afford, the Russian vine, *Polygonum baldschuanicum*, is really spectacular with its great feathery sprays of white flowers in late summer. Let this one compete with the weeds if there is space on a bank for its untrammelled growth.

The climbing *Hydrangea petiolaris* attaches itself to walls and trees by adventitious roots. Consigned to growing flat on the ground, these roots will change their function to that of not only anchoring the plant in place but of turning it into a colony. The side growths, rather thicker and more substantial than those of most climbing plants, will attempt to grow upwards before resorting to a more prostrate position, building up a mass of hummocky growth 60cm (24in) or more above ground level.

Although it has no scent I am very fond of the everlasting pea, *Lathyrus latifolius*, for it is a reminder of the peace and charm of an old cottage garden. I planted a few seedlings – it is as easy to raise as is the sweet pea in this way – against a bush laburnum and against the bole of a silver birch, here to compete with and furnish the base of a 'Dorothy Perkins' rose growing up against it. In both cases the pea goes upwards where it can get a hold; otherwise it sprawls across the ground, oblivious to other plants and weeds which may arise. This makes me wonder if it could be used for actually combating weeds, although it is herbaceous in habit.

With any of these sprawling climbing plants relegated to trailing, it helps to accelerate complete coverage if initially one spreads out the main growths so that they do not all tend to follow the same line and bunch up. If they are then pegged in position they will root more speedily and the growths will not be in competition with their own kind. Like the stronger ivies they can be well spaced out with planting distances of up to 2·5m (8ft) apart, but even more space can be given if one is willing to wait a little longer for fulfilment.

RAMPANT ROSES

Any strong-growing rambling or trailing rose is worth a trial. One of the best to employ for this purpose is *Rosa* × *paulii*: it not only trails but forms mounds of interlacing branches sufficient to quell most weeds, and it is very liberal with its bunches of single white, scented flowers. My next choice would be *R.* 'Max Graf', which is much more confined in spread but which creeps and roots to form a fairly low thicket. This has single pink, fragrant flowers. *R. wichuraiana*, involved in the ancestry of so many of the garden ramblers, holds its foliage for much of the winter and is also good for the purpose. *R. multiflora*, with small, fragrant white flowers in large heads, will trail and form a dense low thicket. So too will the pale pink *R.* 'Macrantha' and its forms, of which 'Raubritter' is one of the most delightful.

These are a few of the outstanding types obtainable if one visits a nursery offering a good selection of rose species and shrub roses. The alternative it to pin one's faith on one or two of the most vigorous garden ramblers like 'Albertine', 'Alberic Barbier', 'American Pillar' and 'Wedding Day', and assist them with a periodic foray to remove any strong weeds which force their way through.

Distances from 2·5m (8ft) apart up to 3m (10ft) or more for the very vigorous *R.* × *paulii*, should prove satisfactory. The early growths can again be guided in the way they should go and pruning need consist of little more than the removal of any dead wood which menaces the mass. They should be cut hard back after planting to encourage the right type of strong young growths from the base.

AN ARCHANGEL IN NAME ONLY

I am full of admiration for the variegated archangel, *Lamiastrum galeobdolon* 'Variegatum' (*Lamium galeobdolon* 'Variegata'), which today is often lauded as an excellent, quick ground coverer for all and sundry. Here I must give a word of warning that it should not be used for general purposes in the average home garden, for it will be forever vigorously competing with its neighbours. But where space is available away from choice plants, it is an admirable subject.

Capable of making 90cm (36in) or more of growth in a season it can be planted rather more than this distance apart and will link up very quickly, forming a low carpet of silver-mottled, evergreen leaves of considerable charm which are especially valued in the winter. It roots as it goes, and stem cuttings will put forth roots in a few days, so there is little expense involved in planting it fairly closely to get quick results. It prefers shade, is quite happy where shade is most dense, and will make a splendid low carpet beneath trees or large shrubs in any type of soil, provided it remains reasonably moist.

FOR WET GROUND

All willows love moist and boggy ground, and several of the prostrate growing forms can be used for ground cover. The best and least rampant is the creeping willow, *Salix repens*, with small greyish-green leaves, but I prefer its variety, *argentea*, which has much more silvery foliage. In the early years after planting, great care should be taken to shorten back long slender shoots to encourage side growths and obtain quicker, complete coverage.

FOR DRY SHADE

In the dense shade beneath trees only a small proportion of the rain which falls in summer may reach the ground. A measure of surface drought may prevail from midsummer until leaf-fall, especially beneath trees like elm and silver birch which produce mats of surface-feeding roots. Here even drenching the ground by artificial watering during prolonged drought will benefit plants growing beneath for a day or two only and then it has to be repeated, for one is also providing moisture for the trees and their requirements are prodigious.

Complete shade can be borne by many plants if there is adequate moisture present but comparatively few will establish themselves and thrive in both shade and drought. We have already discussed some and all will be gathered together in a complete list in the next chapter. The ivies fit in here; and there are two other rampant ground coverers to add.

For indifference to such adversities and for rapid growth the unarmed bramble, *Rubus tricolor*, is hard to beat. This is quick to establish itself and to start making up to 2·5m (8ft) of growth each season, so it can be well spaced out. It has furry reddish-brown stems and dark green glossy leaves covered beneath with a whitish felt. While its small white flowers and edible red fruits may be of little consequence, the stems and leaves on the dense plants which build themselves up into low mounds, make an attractive feature in places where space is not at a premium and where growing conditions are not of the best.

Completely different in all its parts but of the same enduring nature, is *Trachystemon orientalis* which is bedevilled with the synonymous names of *Borago orientalis*, *Nordmannia cordifolia* and *Psilostemon orientalis*. This does not necessarily need shade or dry soil but is quite unaffected by them. It spreads by means of thick rhizomes just beneath or on the surface of the soil. The foliage dies away completely during the winter, then from mid-March onwards spikes of blue flowers push forth before the new leaves appear. These leaves are large, as much as 30cm (12in) long and 20cm (8in) across, deep green and hairy; and they form a well-nigh impenetrable barrier to weeds. Although a rampant forager, the plant is not insidious, for the signs of trespassing rhizomes are soon detected and their size is such that there is no difficulty in completely removing them where a check is necessary. A reasonable distance to plant is 75cm (30in) apart.

REFRACTORY INVADERS

These can be the problem plants and it is doubtful whether two of the following three subjects have any place in the average home garden; but I feel that I ought to mention them for they do appear in many a nurseryman's catalogue. Snow-in-summer, *Cerastium tomentosum*, may be permissible, although it is already in possession in many a small garden, largely because it has been regarded as a rockery plant and so placed. A rough, rocky bank, not the more hallowed precincts of a rock-garden should be its home, for without doubt it is a marauder, spreading its underground stems insidiously under and between rocks and plants, stems which are most difficult to extract. Otherwise, with its silvery-grey leaves and masses of white flowers, it is a plant of considerable beauty and character.

Beware of that other beautiful menace, the winter heliotrope, *Petasites fragrans*. How charming and desirable it seems when its spikes of mauve and white, delightfully scented flowers appear above the bare earth in February, and what good ground cover its large rounded leaves make during the whole of the summer. But beneath the surface its underground stems spread avariciously in all directions and are almost as difficult to extract properly as those of the notorious couch-grass. For all this it does an excellent job in nature in clothing cliffs and banks, but with few exceptions it is a plant to be avoided for the garden.

On several occasions I have seen the dwarf bamboo, *Arundinaria vagans*, lauded as a ground-cover plant for the home garden. I would agree with this, but only when there is adequate space and a densely shaded area beneath trees, or a rough bank, to clothe. It certainly makes a beautiful light green mass up to 90cm (36in) high; but it goes on spreading regardless of those around and it should be introduced to a garden only after its virtues have been weighed carefully against its vices.

CHAPTER FIFTEEN

PLANTS FOR DIFFERENT SOILS AND SITUATIONS

The lists in this chapter will be useful for ascertaining at a glance the most suitable plants for a particular soil or situation. They cover only those plants which have been mentioned in the preceding chapters; thus in most cases I have been able to use just the generic name to cover all the species mentioned. It must not be assumed that other species outside the range of this book will likewise flourish in these particular conditions. For instance, *Euphorbia* appears under the heading of plants for dry shade and is meant to include just the one species mentioned: *E. robbiae*. The majority of other garden euphorbias prefer full sun.

A number of genera appear under more than one type of soil heading which shows that they are very adaptable. Those which are not included in any of the soil lists will generally grow in any reasonably good garden soil. Any slight preferences will have been mentioned in the preceding text. If a plant does not appear under any of the shade lists, it is because it probably prefers the sun. If it does equally well in semi-shade or sun, this will probably have been mentioned previously.

FOR HEAVY CLAY SOILS

This selection includes only those plants which can be thoroughly relied on to succeed in a soil that has a high clay content, and is extremely sticky and difficult to work. Many of the plants which do not appear under this heading may well succeed in a heavy clay-type soil which has been well worked and ameliorated over the years.

Ajuga	*Euphorbia*	*Rosa*
Alchemilla	*Genista*	*Rubus*
Arisarum	*Geranium*	*Salix*
Asarum	*Hedera*	*Sarcococca*
Asperula	*Hosta*	*Saxifraga* × *urbium*
Berberis	*Hypericum*	*Senecio*
Bergenia	*Lamium*	*Symphoricarpos*
Brunnera	*Lonicera*	*Symphytum*
Chaenomeles	*Lysimachia*	*Tellima*
Clematis	*Mahonia*	*Tiarella*
Convallaria	*Nepeta*	*Trachystemon*
Cotoneaster	*Polygonum*	*Vancouveria*
Cotula	*Potentilla*	*Viburnum*
Cytisus	*Primula*	*Vinca*
Doronicum	*Prunella*	*Waldsteinia*
Epimedium	*Prunus*	
Euonymus	*Pulmonaria*	

REQUIRING A LIME-FREE SOIL

Generally one thinks in terms of plenty of humus, in the form of peat or leaf-mould, in conjunction with lime-free or acid soils. This is not always highly important but it is very desirable for such genera as *Calluna*, *Erica*, *Galax*, *Gaultheria* and *Pernettya*.

Calluna	*Erica*	*Lithospermum*
Chaenomeles	*Galax*	*Pachysandra*
Chamaepericlymenum	*Gaultheria*	*Pernettya*

FOR CHALKY SOILS

Chalky soils are encountered in districts where the underlying formation is limestone. To some plants an alkaline soil is anathema, while others will tolerate it. Where there is a high percentage of lime, the following plants are among the best to employ.

Acaena	*Brunnera*	*Cotoneaster*
Ajuga	*Campanula*	*Cotula*
Alchemilla	*Cerastium*	*Dryas*
Antennaria	*Ceratostigma*	*Epimedium*
Berberis	*Clematis*	*Euonymus*
Bergenia	*Convallaria*	*Euphorbia*

Page 135 (*above*) *Epimedium* × *youngianum* 'Niveum', one of the daintiest of the ground-covering barrenworts; (*below*) *Origanum vulgare* 'Aureum' frames and combines with the deep green foliage and blue flowers of *Brunnera macrophylla* in the author's garden

Page 136 (above) Dense shade and dry soil do not deter the variegated arch-angel, *Lamiastrum galeobdolon* 'Variegatum'; (below) the quite massive foliage of *Trachystemon orientalis* has architectural value as well as ground-covering capacity in shady places

Geranium	Mahonia	Stachys
Hebe	Polygonum	Symphoricarpos
Hedera	Potentilla	Symphytum
Houttuynia	Primula	Tellima
Hypericum	Prunus	Thymus
Juniperus	Pulmonaria	Vancouveria
Lamium	Rubus	Vinca
Lathyrus	Santolina	Viola
Lavandula	Sarcococca	Waldsteinia
Lonicera	Sedum	

FOR DRY SOILS IN FULL SUN

This list is of plants which will stand plenty of sun in one of the lighter well-drained soils which soon become very dry.

Acaena	Dorycnium	Parthenocissus
Antennaria	Euphorbia	Santolina
Arenaria montana	Genista	Sedum
Artemisia	Hebe	Senecio
Cerastium	Herniaria	Stachys
Ceratostigma	Hypericum	Thymus
Chaenomeles	Juniperus	Trachystemon
Chamaemelum	Lathyrus	Viola labradorica
Cotula	Lavandula	
Cytisus	Nepeta	

FOR PLANTING IN POOR SOIL

There may be occasions when it is not practical to provide a reasonable medium for plants to grow in, and one has to look for something with the capacity to thrive where the soil is thin, stony, full of builders' and other rubbish or otherwise impoverished and lacking in any sort of texture. The following plants are likely to succeed under these conditions, but it is helpful to give them a little good soil round the roots when planting to give them a flying start.

Acaena	Campanula poscharskyana	Euphorbia
Ajuga	Cerastium	Genista
Antennaria	Cotula	Hedera
Bergenia	Cytisus	Herniaria

I

Hypericum	*Rubus*	*Sedum spurium*
Pachysandra	*Sagina*	*Thymus drucei*
Polygonum	*Saxifraga* × *urbium*	*Vinca*

FOR A VERY MOIST SOIL

Where the ground is in a continual state of moisture above the average but is not water-logged and boggy, the following plants will thrive best.

Ajuga	*Lysimachia*	*Primula*
Hosta	*Mentha*	*Salix*
Houttuynia	*Polygonum bistorta*	*Symphoricarpos*

FOR DRY SHADE

Beneath a canopy of thick, spreading trees, in the densest parts of woodland where the tree foliage keeps off most of the summer rain and they have to compete with the surface roots of the trees for moisture, the following plants will usually succeed.

Arisarum	*Geranium phaeum*	*Rubus*
Bergenia	*Hedera*	*Sarcococca*
Epimedium	*Hypericum*	*Trachystemon*
Euphorbia	*Lamiastrum*	*Vancouveria*
Galium	*Lonicera pileata*	*Vinca minor*
Gaultheria shallon	*Mahonia*	*Waldsteinia*
Geranium macrorrhizum	*Pachysandra*	

FOR FULL SHADE

The following plants will stand full, even fairly dense shade if they have adequate moisture at the roots. See also the list of plants for dry shade.

Asarum	*Gaultheria procumbens*	*Symphytum*
Euonymus	*Maianthemum*	*Viburnum*
Galax	*Prunus*	

FOR PARTIAL SHADE

This means either very thin shade through which some sunshine can filter or situations where there is some relief from the sun during the hottest part of the day. See also the lists of plants for full and dry shade.

Ajuga reptans 'Variegata'	*Galium*	*Polygonum*
Alchemilla	*Glechoma*	*Potentilla alba*
Arenaria balearica	*Helxine*	*Primula*
Astrantia	*Heuchera*	*Pulmonaria*
Berberis	*Heucherella*	*Saxifraga* × *urbium*
Brunnera	*Hosta*	*Tellima*
Convallaria	*Hydrangea*	*Tiarella*
Cotoneaster	*Lamium*	*Viola* (except
Dicentra	*Lysimachia*	*V. labradorica*)
Doronicum	*Omphalodes*	

FOR COASTAL AREAS

While the air in coastal areas may be good for the human frame it is not always so kind to plants. Depending on the coastline and the degree of exposure to sea breezes and gales, it may contain varying amounts of salt which not all plants like, either above or below ground. The majority of plants do just as well, often even better, in these areas than farther inland if they are not growing too close to the sea or are adequately sheltered from any effect it may have. The following will however survive quite happily under most of the hardships which proximity to the sea brings – some of them even under the full brunt of offshore gales and salt-laden spray.

Acaena	*Calluna*	*Frankenia*
Ajuga	*Campanula*	*Galium*
Alchemilla	*Ceratostigma*	*Genista*
Antennaria	*Clematis*	*Geranium*
Anthemis	*Cotoneaster*	*Hebe*
Arundinaria	*Cytisus*	*Hedera*
Astrantia	*Dryas*	*Heuchera*
Berberis	*Erica*	*Hypericum*
Bergenia	*Euonymus*	*Lathyrus*

Lavandula	*Rubus*	*Stachys*
Lonicera	*Salix*	*Symphoricarpos*
Mahonia	*Santolina*	*Thymus*
Nepeta	*Sarcococca*	*Viburnum*
Polygonum	*Saxifraga*	*Vinca*
Potentilla	*Sedum*	*Waldsteinia*
Rosa	*Senecio*	

FOR INDUSTRIAL AREAS

The degree of atmospheric pollution will vary according to the type, amount and concentration or dispersal of industry. Generally, most of the plants we have been discussing will succeed under normal residential conditions, for the atmospheric pollution arising from the chimneys of dwelling-houses continues to decrease as electricity, gas and oil take over from coal-burning fires. Where there is much heavy industry, however, factory chimneys, fumes, dust and heavy traffic will all add to the impurities in the air. The following plants can be relied on to accept these conditions with the least signs of resentment.

Alchemilla	*Euphorbia*	*Potentilla*
Berberis	*Galium*	*Prunus*
Bergenia	*Genista*	*Rosa*
Campanula	*Geranium*	*Salix*
Chaenomeles	*Hebe*	*Saxifraga* × *urbium*
Cotoneaster	*Hedera*	*Senecio*
Cytisus	*Hydrangea*	*Symphoricarpos*
Dicentra	*Mahonia*	*Tellima*
Doronicum	*Nepeta*	*Vancouveria*
Epimedium	*Parthenocissus*	*Vinca*
Euonymus	*Polygonum*	*Waldsteinia*

PART FOUR

THE ATTACK ON WEEDS

Not every part of the garden can be made inviolate to weeds by thoughtful and deliberate planning and planting; and not every gardener wants much of his garden planted as a more or less permanent foil to weeds. Seasonal bedding, herbaceous borders, fruit or vegetables, and cut-flower subjects like dahlias and chrysanthemums, may be the pride and joy. These are not facets where much self-defence can be employed. Not everyone wants a hard impervious path and even the finest and most flourishing of lawns is wide open to invasion. Defence may be the beginning but it cannot conquer weeds entirely. Inevitably, there will be loopholes in that defence which can be sealed off only by counter-attack. Thus, despite all that has been said before, there is still work to do, however much it has already been reduced; so we shall now turn to ways and means of lightening this particular load.

CHAPTER SIXTEEN

BY MANUAL MEANS

I well remember my earliest days in horticulture when the hand and the hoe were the accepted ways of combating weeds. That the plants themselves were instrumental in smothering weeds was taken for granted, but the term ground cover in its direct application to ornamental horticulture was an uncoined phrase and few thought specifically about the better employment of plants for this purpose. Destruction by chemical means was really only in its infancy: just phenolic substances employed on comparatively rare occasions and sodium chlorate just beginning to be known and used, often with disastrous results.

Science has unearthed and concocted many lethal substances to make weed destruction easier and more thorough, with less backbreaking toil, but they do not – and I suggest never will – entirely eliminate manual means of control. An enlightened policy of no-digging became headlines for a time, then faded into comparative obscurity. Cultivation of the soil, whether deep or surface, is essential for creating a home for plants and for servicing many of them afterwards. Even hoeing is not levied entirely against the weed population. But let us first take a look at the simplest, perhaps almost primitive, method of ousting weeds.

HAND-WEEDING

Long past are the days when Rudyard Kipling wrote:

While better men than we go out and start their working lives?
At grubbing weeds from gravel paths with broken dinner knives.

I am not dwelling in the past when I say that we still have to be prepared to get down on our haunches and pull out weeds with our hands, and that this is not quite the simple menial task that it is generally made out to be. What other method is there of getting rid of weeds in rock-gardens, from in between stones, from among plants growing closely together and from out of the hearts of the plants themselves? What is the last resort when continued wet weather makes the hoe a useless tool and rules out destruction with certain chemicals?

Are there any secrets to make hand-weeding easier? (It could hardly be made more effective.) Not really; it is just a matter of common sense. Bear in mind that it is more difficult to extract the roots if the ground is very firm or dry; and rather messy if it is very wet. Make sure that you get a grip below the crowns of deep-rooted weeds, assisting their extraction with a hand fork if necessary. Those weeds with large fibrous root systems should be shaken from side to side as they are being drawn out; the roots will then come out more cleanly and with less disturbance to the soil. This is very important when one is pulling weeds out of the hearts of plants or from among young seedlings.

DEEP CULTIVATION

Although the main purpose of digging with spade or fork may be to loosen the soil and to prepare it for planting, it is also the time to make the first pre-planting attack on weeds, the time to extract every bit possible of the perennials and to bury deeply any annual weeds which may be present on the surface. The fork is the best tool for winkling out the roots of the perennials; but if there are annual weeds to bury and many weed seeds likely in the surface soil, the spade is better. Use it to skim off the top layer which should be placed right in the bottom of the spit-deep and -wide trench which is so essential to maintain if you are to dig properly, taking care of course in so doing not to bury at the same time any portions of the roots of perennial weeds which may have the capacity to grow again. Getting this top layer well below the surface will account for the weed growth and put a good number of weed seeds below germinating depth; some of these may lose their vitality eventually, especially if the ground is planted with long-term subjects, in which case all so buried will be tucked away for an indefinite period.

SURFACE PREPARATIONS FOR PLANTING

The value of bare fallowing has been drawn to attention in Chapter Six. When the ground is prepared finally this will be the last chance of cleaning it before the plants themselves complicate the issue. Most of the planting of non-woody subjects is done in the spring, and if a prolific crop of weed seedlings is anticipated and planting can be deferred long enough to enable some germination to take place, the first blow can be struck. If the weed seedlings are disturbed by scuffling or hoeing when the surface is dry, and if the ground remains in this state for a couple of days, the majority will be destroyed. Too often one sees weedy ground prepared and planted in one operation.

HOEING

This is another common, simple operation so often done badly. The first thing is the tool for the job. We can forget the draw and triangular hoes except that they are useful tools for drawing out drills for seeds. They had added value when it was the practice to hoe gravelled drives, and they are good for singling mangolds and sugar-beet in the field; but for garden use one must turn to the push type of hoe so that one does not walk over the ground that has been disturbed and tread the weeds back in.

In my opinion it does not matter very much which type of push hoe is used: the main thing is to use it properly and at the right time. There is a choice between the Dutch type, consisting of a blade welded across a pair of prongs, and the Paxton or prongless type where the blade is attached at an angle directly to the neck of the hoe. These are available either in the forms which have existed for years or with a new look, and there are variations from each whereby one hoes with both a forward and backward action, and so on. All in my opinion are equally efficient, given intelligent and sensible handling, and it is a matter of choosing the type and size to suit one's requirements and style of working.

Whatever type it is, unless it is constructed of stainless steel, the hoe will rust and pit badly if it is not cleaned and oiled when not in use. Too few home gardeners care properly for the spade; even fewer for the hoe. A rusted pitted tool will have a short life. It will be harder to push through the soil, and even harder if the soil is wet or sticky when it will cling to the hoe's pitted surface. It should be cleaned, dried and wiped with an oily rag each time it has been used and it should be sharpened as often as necessary.

A surface with no tilth, ie top layer of reasonably loose soil, is difficult to hoe properly. One must get below the surface and cut the weeds off through the roots, not just tear them off at ground level. Hoeing on heavy clay soils in summer can become almost impossible, whether the ground is wet or dry, if there is no tilth to get a bite with the hoe. Thus the extent and the timing of winter cultural operations – such as forking or digging early in the season – to enable frost to break down the surface soil, can have a bearing on the ease and success of manual weed destruction in the months to follow.

Stabbing at the soil is no way to hoe. It is hard on the tool, the hands and muscles of the arm. It is dangerous to adjacent plants and is likely to chop and maul the weeds about rather than separate them cleanly from the soil. The shaft of the hoe can be held and operated at an angle from either below or above the armpit, provided that the blade can be pushed through the soil on a parallel plane with it. The style of working and the height of the operator can have a bearing on the ideal length of shaft to have fitted. It is well worth while weighing up and testing to see if one can work better and more easily with a shaft which is longer or shorter than the average size.

If one acquires the knack of working with the hoe on either side of the body, ie becomes ambidextrous in its use, this not only rests muscles without the need to stop but often enables one to use the tool more easily in difficult places. A good hoer works with strokes that are as long and easy as the circumstances permit and he avoids short stabbing motions as much as possible. By the way in which he brings the hoe back to make the next stroke, he knocks the weeds free and leaves them loose on the surface, not half-buried.

All the skill and ease in manipulating a hoe will be lost, however, if the timing is not right. A good gardener works with and not in defiance of the weather, if it is humanly possible to do so. He tries to hoe when the soil is reasonably dry on top and when the sun is shining to scorch and finish off the weeds. If he is obliged to operate at a less opportune time, he takes care to rake or pick off at least the largest of the weeds so that they will not take root again.

Small cultivators, either hand or mechanically propelled, are available to reduce hand labour. Their use in the garden is confined to those parts such as the fruit and vegetable areas, where the planting is in straight rows sufficiently spaced to permit a cultivator to operate comfortably. Even there the hoe is not displaced entirely, for one cannot cultivate ground mechanically right up to the plants. It is doubtful therefore whether these implements are of widespread value to the home gardener.

BURNING OFF

Before herbicides really came into prominence, the flame-gun was evolved as an alternative to the hoe. It had its spell of publicity, is still with us and is a useful tool, but naturally, there are limitations to its use. It can seldom be employed safely between plants except perhaps for shrubs with plenty of open ground still between them, and then great care must be taken not to scorch low branches or main stems at ground level.

It was on paths and for burning down rough rubbish where there was nothing else to harm, that its main use lay in its short heyday; and there are times when it can still be an appropriate tool for these purposes. Small hand or larger wheeled types are available, and the knack of using the flame-gun, if there is an appreciable amount of green top growth to destroy, is not to attempt to burn this right down in one operation. This takes too long. It is better by far to go over the ground twice: the first time to scorch and kill the top growth, and again a few days later when it has died and dried somewhat, when it will be reduced to ashes more readily. The other advantage of the flame-gun, and perhaps its greatest asset, is that the heat will also destroy most of the weed seeds lying on the surface.

Needless to say, a tool with a fierce flame and engendering a considerable amount of direct heat, must be lit and handled strictly according to the maker's instructions; and in plying the flame-gun one must never forget that there will be intense heat beyond the limits of the actual flame, quite sufficient to scorch tender young growths severely.

MULCHING

A mulch is a loose layer of material created or placed on the surface of the ground primarily for the purpose of conserving moisture. This in itself, together with any nutriment which an added mulch may provide, assists indirectly in weed-control by promoting the growth of the plants and more complete coverage of the ground. A mulch can, however, keep down weeds directly.

First I shall refer again to cultivating and hoeing and the creation of a loose layer of soil on the surface, known as a tilth. This is a form of mulch in that the loose layer, when it dries, will effectively check capillarity in the soil, ie the upward movement of water culminating in evaporation from the surface. Thus a tilth is a conserver of moisture and by its creation weeds are destroyed.

To be fully effective against weeds the mulch needs to be of sufficient depth to prevent weed seeds from germinating and to be in itself devoid of such seeds. A mulch of moss peat not less than 2·5 cm (1 in) thick is probably the most suitable material, but it is not cheap to apply at this rate. Partially rotted leaves free from any adulteration are the next best bet, and here I must refer again to my practice of letting autumn leaves lie wherever I can, pinning them down with a light dressing of some heavier mulching material, which could well be peat. This substance on its own takes a long time to rot down into plant food and will not provide any immediate nourishment to plants.

Sawdust, spent hops and chopped straw and bracken are other useful sterile materials. There used to be strong opposition to adding sawdust to the soil, but this has now been confounded. It is good for the purpose, although it is rather inclined to cake after heavy rain. The other three materials are light and loose, and liable to blow about until they have become well bedded down. If they are readily available and cheap, the ideal would be to compromise by adding peat to make them more stable. Such materials will rot down much quicker than peat on its own and thus also provide plant food. They will need topping up periodically to maintain a seal against the germination of weed seeds.

Pulverised bark is a substance which is coming to the fore now for mulching purposes. As with sawdust, anything of a woody nature applied to the soil has long been viewed with suspicion as a likely source of fungus infection of some kind, but thoughts have changed. Enormous quantities of bark stripped from timber used in the building industry, in paper-mills etc have posed problems of disposal. Pulverised into various grades, the finest is of similar texture to peat and makes an ideal substitute, being sterile, a good weed-suppressor and conserver of soil moisture. As with peat, a dressing 2·5cm (1in) thick is really essential to suppress the germination of weeds in the soil beneath.

Well-rotted farmyard manure – preferably from horses – and compost will provide the most sustenance for plants if this is also an object of the exercise, but it is difficult to guarantee either of these substances being free from weed seeds. Nevertheless, they can still be quite effective and prevent more weeds than they introduce. If weed seeds are present, most of them will germinate in the mulch and the roots of the seedlings will have to find their way into the ground beneath before they can become firmly established. A mulch, while it is still loose, soon dries out; and if it is stirred during dry sunny weather the tender young seedlings will soon wilt away. Despite this, one's aim should always be to use weed-free mulches if suitable material is available, otherwise the objective will be partially defeated.

Weed suppression by mulching with heavy-grade black polythene stretched over the surface of the ground – through which plants can be inserted with as little fracturing of the polythene as possible – is becoming more widely adopted in commercial establishments. It holds some possibilities for the home gardener, although its use is rather limited. It is not easy to handle nor is it pleasant to look at round ornamental plants, but in the vegetable garden one may well practise with it on crops like potatoes and members of the cabbage tribe which lend themselves more to this form of weed-control. The polythene must be laid flat on clean ground, which has been raked down to a fine tilth in the spring, when it will also help to conserve soil moisture and raise the temperature of the soil with additionally beneficial results.

CHAPTER SEVENTEEN

CHEMICAL WEED-CONTROL

To continue my opening remarks in the previous chapter: when I started in horticulture over forty years ago the destruction of weeds by chemical means anywhere other than on paths and drives was barely contemplated. Arsenical and phenolic substances were occasionally employed; but these did little more than burn off the top growth. Sodium chlorate was just coming into use and was being recognised as a rather more total and longer-lasting destroyer. Its inflammability when it had dried on the treated weeds, or on the clothing of the operator, was known; but in my experience, it was not taken as seriously as it ought to have been. More important, however, its penetrating powers and possible side effects were not fully known and appreciated.

The first really notable advance in weed-control with chemicals was the introduction of selective weedkillers for grass surfaces. These are now accepted as the standard means of control and, to a large extent, they have settled down into a fairly stable pattern. With increasing labour problems in professional circles, attention then turned to the use of chemicals for destroying weeds in cultivated ground without harm to the rightful occupants; and over the past decade there have been startling advances in this and in chemical weed-control generally.

The range of substances employed is considerable and is forever increasing. Many are not yet available to the home gardener, unless of course he has contacts with the professional grower and can obtain them from behind the counter. Here I must give a word of warning. There is good reason for officially confining their distribution through the open market, for many of them require great care and attention in application and their full potential, their side and after effects are still being investigated. Unless therefore one becomes very well versed in the use of any particular substance which is outside the range officially available to the amateur gardener, and is meticulous in handling and applying it in accordance with recommendations, one should not dabble with substances confined to professional users whose areas of operation are vastly different from that of the home garden.

At this point I feel it desirable to emphasise that, while the home gardener can with care in choice and application use weed-killers quite safely on paths, lawn and in waste places, he should approach their use between plants with a great deal of caution. In such situations weedkillers are not easy to apply at the right dosage and without damaging the plants, some of which may be more susceptible to injury than others. If he wishes to embark on this form of weed-control, say among his shrubs and roses, he should do so on a limited scale at first to satisfy himself that he can master the techniques of application and that his plants will come through unharmed.

There is available to the amateur gardener a range of well-tried substances adequate for his needs. Indeed I have found it desirable to reduce this range somewhat in order to make the pattern of control more readily understood. For obvious reasons I have confined myself to naming the active ingredient only, omitting the trade names under which most of the substances are distributed.

With the advance in this field weedkillers were officially designated 'herbicides', a title which will be much used in the notes to follow. Unless otherwise stated, the substances are applied in solution in accordance with the maker's instructions. Rates of application are not given, for these vary with the proprietary brand.

HERBICIDES APPLIED TO EXISTING WEEDS

I   TOTAL

(a) *Contact killers*   These kill all green top growth with which they come in contact. Their action upon the roots and woody parts of a plant is confined to the weakening effects from the death of that top growth, which will be more accentuated by continued destruction of any new stems and leaves subsequently put forth. Thus, by persistent application to prevent perennial weeds from regaining their vigour, ultimate destruction may eventually ensue but, as we shall learn later, there are quicker and more effective ways of achieving this.

Obviously, the more top growth there is, the more effective the treatment will appear to be. Generally, however, it is not advisable to wait for substantial growth before acting – especially as regards annual weeds, some of which start seeding very early. Herbicides generally do not destroy weed seeds, so one of the prime aims must be to prevent seeding. Furthermore, treating an abundance of top growth increases the danger of spreading the herbicide more widely and on to neighbouring plants, especially when the operation is done by means of pressure spraying. Moreover, the sight of dead weeds for weeks on end is unpleasant to say the least. One must therefore choose the optimum time for application when the majority of seeds near the surface will have germinated and the top growth as a whole is not too advanced.

The old phenolic substances have been mentioned and these are still available, but in general they have been superseded by para-quat and diquat which are usually combined in a mixture under various trade names. The great advantage of these paraquat/diquat mixtures is that they become inactive on contact with the soil and so there is no residual danger: indeed, planting and sowing can normally be carried out twenty-four hours after application. They can be applied in practically any weather, except when it is actually raining or the foliage is already wet: conditions in which the herbicide may be either washed off or greatly diluted. Rain within a short time after application does not usually reduce their effectiveness.

(b) *Translocated killers*   These are taken in by the foliage and move through the plant's system. Thus they are capable of destroying the roots of perennial weeds. The main one employed is sodium chlorate, which has already been mentioned as a herbicide of long standing and one with certain dangerous properties. One of these, inflammability when it dries, has now been countered with a fire-reducing additive and one should use only those brands which have been made safe in this way. There remains, however, the risk of contamination of the soil by penetration, making it unfit for the growth of plants for several months; and also a sideways movement of the substance in the soil, thus placing at risk plants which are growing alongside the areas treated with the substance, even though the roots of these may not be actually penetrating the immediate danger zone. The proximity of plants, especially trees and shrubs with widely penetrating roots, must be taken into account before one resorts to the use of sodium chlorate; and it is best confined to drives and paths where there are no closely adjacent plants and to open areas which have to be cleared of persistent weeds, and where a time-lag of not less than six months before planting can be given.

Ammonium sulphamate, with very similiar properties to those of sodium chlorate, is also available but not so widely used. Personally, I would counsel the home gardener to consider them only as a last resort if other safer chemicals will not serve his purpose.

Where couch and other grasses are the main problem, dalapon at a high dosage rate can be used, applied when the grasses are in vigorous growth. A time-lag of about two months is then necessary before any planting can be carried out.

2   SELECTIVE

A selective herbicide is one which kills only the weeds and not the plants among which they are growing, either because it is one of the substances which, when applied in low doses, has this selective action or is more truly selective in that for various reasons certain plants are resistant. It has therefore no effect unless the plants receive an extra strong dose, in which case some damage, generally of a temporary nature, may occur. As before, I have divided these herbicides into two classes.

(a) *Contact killers*   The ordinary selective lawn herbicides cannot be applied safely to a newly sown or turved lawn for six months after sowing or laying, during which time broad-leaved weeds may flourish and seriously undermine the limited resistance of the young grasses. Two other herbicides, ioxynil and morfamquat, are however safe to use after the young grasses have made their second leaves and also among onions and leeks when a

K

similar stage in growth has been reached. Ioxynil should not be used on a lawn containing crested dog's-tail-grass in the seed mixture. Morfamquat is safe to use during the first six months after a lawn has been laid with turves.

(b) *Translocated killers* Here we have the selective lawn herbicides so widely used. Many of them have complicated chemical names which are simplified by the use of single letters and numerals by which they are now universally known. All have a similar effect on broad-leaved weeds, causing them to sit up, to twist and curl before dying; a process which may take up to three weeks. When they are applied correctly in the right conditions, the roots of the weeds will also be killed; but if for any reason the treatment has not been fully effective and there has been some aftergrowth, a second application about six weeks after the first may be necessary.

The most popular of these herbicides is still 2,4-D, which is very effective against daisies, dandelions and plantains; as also is MCPA. Yarrow, clover, trefoil, mouse-ear chickweed and pearlwort with smaller leaves or a persistent creeping habit are rather more difficult, and for these one should use mecoprop or dichlorprop. There are proprietary brands of selective lawn weedkillers which contain both 2,4-D and dichlorprop, and these give the widest control.

Some of these herbicides are now available in granular form combined with lawn fertilisers. While I personally prefer to apply a selective herbicide in liquid form to ensure quicker and more complete absorption by the leaves, and consider that fertilising leads to more effective weed-control if carried out about ten days previously, these combined mixtures do have the advantage of being easier to apply and they are safer in that the dangers of spray drift are avoided. Care should be taken to ensure that they are not mistakenly used for fertilising other plants.

The herbicide 2,4,5-T, either on its own or combined with 2,4-D, is a rather powerful selective one which is used largely to kill brambles, brushwood, nettles etc on rough ground. It should be used for this purpose only in places where there is no spraydrift danger to neighbouring plants. It is powerful enough to kill the stumps of undergrowth, suckers from trees etc after thay have been cut at ground level; also tree-stumps and trees themselves if the bark is slashed round the base to enable the killer to penetrate. While it will not normally affect trees whose bark is intact, it should be kept clear of young specimens and any whose bark has been damaged recently in any way, such as from gnawing by rabbits or by impact from mowing-machines.

Dalapon applied in low doses can be used as a selective herbicide to control couch and other grasses among fruit-trees and shrubs, but not if broad-leaved, softer plants are also present.

HERBICIDES APPLIED TO THE SOIL

These are translocated in action, entering the weeds by absorption through the roots. They will kill shallow rooting weeds already present, but as the top growth of these may prevent much of the herbicide from reaching the soil, to be fully effective application should be made to bare ground with the prime purpose of destroying weed seedlings as they germinate. Thus March and early April are normally the best times of the year to apply these herbicides. To obtain the right penetration, the soil should be reasonably moist at the time of application.

I TOTAL

(a) *Residuals applied in high doses* The substance most widely used for this purpose is simazine which, when applied in high doses to paths and other places where there is no planting, will keep the ground clear of weeds for a whole year. Subsequent annual applications can usually be made at lower dosage rates and still be effective. Simazine remains in the top layer of soil; thus it has no effect on deep-rooted perennial weeds other than at germinating time. It is important not to disturb the surface of the ground, otherwise the protective seal will be broken and germinating weeds may then be able to thrust their roots into the untreated ground beneath. Although it is generally applied in solution, at least one firm offers it in granular form.

Of rather more recent introduction, dichlobenil is used in granular form and is very easy to apply. With all granular herbicides, rain after application will accelerate and increase their effectiveness; but there is more danger than with solutions of very heavy early rains washing the material on to adjacent land, especially when it is applied to a slope. Unlike simazine, dichlo-benil is effective against many of the deeper-rooted perennial weeds like dandelions and docks, horse-tail, thistles and ground elder. It will give a control of up to twelve months when applied in these higher doses in the spring. There should be a time-lag of around twelve months before sowing or planting takes place.

(b) *Partial residuals*   Sodium chlorate, in addition to being a herbicide which kills by translocation through the top growth, can also be used to act via the roots. Unlike residuals described earlier, it washes down gradually through the soil, so its period of control is shorter and a second application during the growing season may be necessary. If it is used for clearing land of strong-growing persistent weeds and grasses, a period of at least six months should elapse before sowing or planting are carried out there.

2   SELECTIVE

(a) *Residuals applied in low doses*   Simazine applied at low dosage rates in the spring can be used to kill germinating weeds between roses, trees and shrubs and fruit-trees and bushes. It is important however to remember that this substance should not be used around small bushes or those which have been planted recently, and that some ornamentals may be damaged by it. The directions as to the limitations in its use which are usually supplied by the makers, should be followed closely. There must be no disturbance of the soil after application, otherwise the weed barrier will be broken. Simazine should therefore be applied to ground which is free of all top growth of weeds, for if any are present and do not succumb ultimately, they will have to be removed afterwards. This cannot be done without disturbing the soil, unless it is possible to burn them off with paraquat without damage to other plants. Simazine should not be used around herbaceous and similar non-woody plants, or on very light soils where it may penetrate too deeply.

Dichlobenil is recommended for use around roses, fruit-trees and bushes, and ornamental trees and shrubs. Despite its greater ease of application in granular form, great care is still essential when it is applied around growing plants, for if the granules are spread too widely or lodge on the leaves of plants, damage will occur. The capacity of dichlobenil to deal not only with germinating weed seedlings but also with perennials, including those of a deep-rooted nature, calls for some circumspection before using it indiscriminately around ornamental trees and shrubs. It is recognised that certain species are susceptible, so any warnings as to limitations in its use provided by the makers must be followed closely. It should certainly not be used around very young or newly planted stock. February and March are the times to apply it to cultivated ground, before the buds of the woody subjects have started to move; preferably not in warm weather when, being somewhat volatile, some of its value may be lost and its period of effectiveness – normally up to six months at these lower dosage rates – is reduced somewhat.

(b) *Pre-emergent herbicides*   These are substances which can be applied to the soil after a crop has been sown, to control germinating weed seedlings which usually spring up at the same time and compete strongly with the crop as it germinates.

They have a limited use in the home garden. Propachlor granules can be used in the vegetable garden, applied after onions, leeks and members of the cabbage tribe have been sown; or in the established herbaceous border in spring to give effective control of germinating weeds for a period of six to eight weeks. A weed-free surface at the time of application is necessary. This early control, although for a limited period, is instrumental in freeing young plants from competition and enabling them to grow stronger and sturdier. It puts paid to that early crop of annual weeds which, if not eliminated, will soon be on a reproduction course resulting in another crop of weeds later in the season.

MOSS DESTROYERS

Moss is very little affected by most of the herbicides commonly used to destroy other weeds, certainly on lawns where it is a frequent and persistent invader. Even in places where total weed-killers can be used, it may be virtually immune or very resistant to them. Ferrous (iron) sulphate applied in conjunction with sulphate of ammonia, with sand as a spreader, has been in use as a lawn weedkiller for as long as I can remember. It destroys both moss and broad-leaved weeds, but although it is still in use today it has lost its time-honoured place to selective weedkillers (although these have no effect on moss).

Mercurous chloride, either alone or combined with ferrous sulphate, gives a more lasting control. A newer chemical, chloroxuron, is claimed to be non-toxic to humans and animals, easy to use, inexpensive, safe to the grasses and remaining effective for a much longer period, thus taking care of many of the moss spores which germinate subsequently. The effective suppression of moss in lawns is however bound up very largely with soil and other conditions, and methods of maintenance, and will be dealt with in a later chapter.

LOOKING TO THE FUTURE

I am conscious of the fact that this chapter is rather the odd man out in that, while the rest of the information in this book will not date rapidly, there is constant research to find or evolve substances which are more or equally efficacious, but easier and safer to handle and apply. The more complex the subject becomes, the greater is the need for closer scrutiny and for more searching tests before the results of research can be truly categorised and the products passing these tests be made available to all.

I had thought of contemplating the near future and attempting to prophesy what other herbicides will soon become available, in that they are already in use by commercial growers but have not yet been marketed for the amateur gardener. On reflection I have come to the conclusion that perhaps it would be unwise to do so, for no matter how promising a certain substance may appear to be, some fault may yet be revealed to delay or cancel out its general release; or before it has had time to really justify itself, another challenger may suddenly appear: so fast is the pace of research. Over and above this, the substance may have all the attributes for widespread use but be difficult or uneconomic to be put on the market in small packs.

I must therefore be content with the status quo, feeling fairly sure that the substances I have described are well established and unlikely to fade out completely for several years. The exponents of herbicidal weed-control in a small way should however always keep in touch with progress and be ready to explore the possibilities of any new aids which may come their way. These people should take the precaution, as with all garden chemicals, of using the products of the most reputable companies only and testing them out in a small way, under specific conditions, before putting them to more widespread use.

CHAPTER EIGHTEEN

HANDLING AND APPLYING HERBICIDES

The use of chemicals of any description, for any purpose or in any sphere, must always be accompanied by the question: 'How safe are they to what they are intended to help or protect, and how safe also to those handling and dispensing them?' Too many have found to their cost that many of the chemicals used in horticulture have dangerous properties: some to a mild degree only; others much greater, even lethal. Safety in their use is largely a matter of carefulness and common sense. Were this not so, it is extremely unlikely that they would ever be placed on the market for all and sundry to employ.

Today, those chemicals used to assist in propagation, nutrition, control of plant growth and the control of pests, diseases and weeds are almost bewildering in their range and often complex in nature. One should never apply such artificial aids and remedies without full knowledge of their action and their potency; and this is particularly so in the destruction of weeds by chemical means, for here 'destruction' is the operative word, whether it be selective or complete. Obviously, what is lethal to one plant is also likely to destroy or severely damage others, so great care in application is necessary from the start. It is also important to know whether any substance could be dangerous to humans or animals. Never, therefore, treat any garden chemicals, especially those of a liquid nature, in a cavalier fashion. Some may be comparatively safe and easy to use, but it is better by far to treat all of them with circumspection and to have the same code of handling for those with the least, as for those with the highest, danger potential.

HANDLING AND STORING

1 Read carefully any information relating to safe use given by the makers on the label or package. Note particularly whether or not the substance is classed as a poison. Of the substances dealt with in the previous chapter, only paraquat and those substances containing mercury are so classed. If any of these substances are to be stored for future use, an extra large label with the word 'Poison' written on it in large red letters is an added precaution.

2 Always store in a cool, dry, frostproof place away from food materials, fertilisers and seeds and out of the reach of children and animals, preferably in a locked cupboard.

3 Keep in the proper containers, tightly closed. Avoid transferring to other containers, especially bottles which have contained soft drinks. If for some reason transference of partly used herbicide to a more substantial container is desirable, remove all old labels and affix new ones with the words 'Weedkiller: Dangerous' clearly printed on them.

4 Destroy all empty containers, those of paper, cardboard or plastic, by burning. Most metal and glass containers can usually be put in the rubbish bin for collection in the usual way, but if one is in any doubt as to the advisability of this, they should be buried at least 45 cm (18in) deep in an out-of-the-way place where they will not be disturbed again. First flatten the metal containers to reduce their bulk. Never clean and re-use the containers for the storage of similar or other substances.

5 Although not all substances are skin irritants or present danger in this way, and not all skins are allergic, it is always a wise precaution to wear rubber gloves, if for no other purpose than to keep the chemicals from going under the fingernails where it is more difficult to thoroughly cleanse. When handling and applying substances with a strong smell or of a volatile nature, and especially when using pressure appliances, protection to prevent the chemicals or any fumes given off from getting to the nose or eyes may be advisable, especially if one has respiratory or optical weaknesses.

6   Wear old clothing. After handling and applying chemicals, wash thoroughly, with hot soapy water, the hands and other parts of the body which have been exposed. Boots and trousers in particular may become contaminated; these should also be washed if necessary.

CHOOSING THE RIGHT APPLIANCE

The types and sizes of appliances are numerous. The majority are designed primarily for the application of insecticides and fungicides, ejecting with a fine, mist-like spray under pressure generated by pumping when in action or built up pneumatically within the appliance by prior pumping. While such sprayers can, with care in use, aided perhaps by a hood over the nozzles to direct the fluid in a downward direction, be used for the application of herbicides, generally I would not go so far as to recommend them to the home gardener for this purpose. Apart from the danger of spray drift by pressure application there is a temptation to use such appliances for the dual purpose of pest and disease control and weedkilling, when the slightest neglect in cleansing after they have been used against weeds can result subsequently in damage to plants.

I stand by the watering-can with dribble or sprinkler bar attached in preference to a rose, and recommend that such a can be kept solely for this purpose and not be used also for watering plants. Dribble or sprinkler bars are quite cheap, are available in several sizes and may be either T-shaped for use on lawns or paths, or narrowly L-shaped for greater ease of application between plants. Some firms now sell plastic applicators complete with different spray bars, and these are ideal for the purpose. Even if reserved for herbicide application, the can or applicator and its parts should be thoroughly cleansed after use, especially if used for both selective and non-selective herbicides.

The ordinary hand-operated sprayer, pneumatic or otherwise, can be used with greater safety on a lawn but again there must be care to avoid spray drift, especially adjacent to beds and borders. A nozzle emitting the spray in a fan rather than in the usual cone is better for herbicide application. Wheeled sprayers specially designed for the application of lawn weedkillers are much safer, but generally the home gardener has insufficient turf area to justify the purchase of a rather costly item such as this. After all, herbicidal treatment of lawns should at the most be necessary only twice in a season; and in the majority of gardens a watering-can or applicator with a good, wide sprinkler bar will perform the job in a reasonable time and with much more safety.

MIXING AND APPLYING

1 Ascertain the right herbicide to use. (See preceding chapter.)
2 Read carefully any instructions given by the makers on the label.
3 Choose the right time of the year to apply the herbicide. (See preceding chapter.)
4 Choose the right weather. Rain to moisten the soil beforehand may be desirable for soil-applied herbicides, and rain immediately following the application will do no harm, even accelerate its action, provided it is not torrential, resulting in flooding of the treated area to carry the herbicide and damage adjacent plants. On slopes where there is a greater danger of this occurring – if the weather is such that thunderstorms are a possibility – where the substance has been applied dry, some light watering in will help to 'fix' it in the treated ground. Wet foliage at the time of application or rain within a few hours afterwards will so dilute or wash off herbicides applied to weed growth as to render them only partially effective.
5 When diluting measure carefully the correct amount of the herbicide to mix with a given volume of water: never guess. If the cap of the container is not stated to be a measure get a properly graduated one. Never rely on spoons, for these can vary in size, whether they be tea, dessert or table. Cleanse the measure thoroughly afterwards, if it is to be used again.
6 Apply the correct amount of herbicide to a given area. When in solution remember that, whatever the dilution rate, it is the amount of active ingredient which matters, not the total amount when diluted, provided that the diluted material is sufficient in quantity to be distributed evenly over that area.

This will be governed by the type of appliance used, and it may be necessary to increase or decrease slightly the recommended amount of water in accordance with the capacity of appliance to eject. To assess this, a trial run over the measured area using clean water only, will help one to gauge the best dilution to use in accordance with the covering capacity of the appliance.

7 Do not mix two herbicides together for a dual purpose unless you are very sure this can be done without adverse interaction and without damage to garden plants by contact or through soil poisoning. Better by far to use herbicides which have already been combined for this purpose, eg 2,4-D with mecoprop or dichlorprop for wider weed destruction on lawns; 2,4-D with 2,4,5-T for use against brushwood and nettles; or simazine and aminotriazole to kill both existing and germinating weeds.

8 Do not dilute more herbicide with water than is currently needed. An excess may not keep for another time, or may be difficult to store with safety, so it will have to be disposed of where it can do no harm to plants or animals.

9 Never mix herbicides or fill appliances at the kitchen sink.

10 Select the right appliance to use.

11 When applying liquid herbicides, do not splash or spray them about carelessly. Be especially careful in the vicinity of plants, and take care not to overstep the edges of the area to be treated. Try to avoid overlapping when treating in strips or sections, for not only will there be waste of material, but in the case of selective herbicides on a lawn an extra dose may cause some browning of the grass. For the same reason turn off the nozzles of a sprayer or avoid dribbles from a watering-can when pausing in the operation. When using wettable powders which are apt to settle, occasionally agitate by shaking to keep them in suspension. Try to avoid walking over a treated area, for in this way herbicide may be carried on to the lawn.

Be careful in the application of granular herbicides. Too free a distributing action may spread them farther than is intended and on to plants rather than around them. When applying herbicide, whether liquid or granular, by hand or appliance, to a large area like a lawn, string off the lawn into strips of a convenient width and calculate how far along, or how many strips, can be covered with a given weight or volume at the correct dosage.

12 Keep household pets shut up to avoid contact with applied herbicides while these are still wet; but remember that both cats and dogs like to chew rough grass occasionally, and if any grass has been treated, some precautions may have to be taken until the grass starts to collapse and become uninviting. Fish are a different proposition, for they are susceptible to a number of chemicals and great care is necessary when applying a herbicide round a garden pool containing fish to ensure that none finds its way into the water.

13 The careful cleansing of all equipment after use is of prime importance. Any traces of herbicide left in the appliance may start corrosion if it is of metal, and such traces could even prove to be a menace to plants when the appliance is used again for another purpose. Wherever practical, appliances – watering-cans in particular – should be reserved solely for herbicides. After use wash all parts thoroughly with hot water containing detergent, forcing it through the nozzles and rinsing several times with clear water. With sprayers I like to be doubly sure by then taking them to pieces, giving the jets a separate swill out, and forcing water through the hoses before reassembling these working parts.

CHAPTER NINETEEN

PROGRAMMES OF CONTROL

No one can lay down hard and fast rules for much depends on soil and situation, style and nature of planting – in general, on the garden itself and on the ability of the owner to employ any or all of the sundry methods of prevention and control of weeds. The following broad guidelines should however provide a key to the operations necessary for keeping the garden as weed-free as possible with the minimum of back-breaking toil.

CLEANING OF LAND

In the layout of the garden, its extension or any subsequent reconstruction, the great importance to future maintenance of proper cleaning by manual means has been fully stressed in a previous chapter, so we need not go into that again. Such back-breaking toil can however often be alleviated and its effectiveness increased by the proper use of herbicides. Brambles, woody weeds in general, nettles and the stronger, difficult weeds can be given a lethal dose of 2,4,5-T, on its own or in combination with 2,4-D. The stumps of undergrowth and of trees can likewise be killed and although these will usually have to be physically removed to permit cultivation of the ground and planting, the danger of aftergrowth from any portions left in the ground will be eliminated.

If deep-rooted weeds rather than woody plants are the main problem, sodium chlorate or ammonium sulphamate can be applied, if one remembers that a period of not less than six months must elapse before the ground can be safely planted. Dalapon may be the answer if couch and strong grasses are the main weeds to be cleared. If the chief concern is annual weeds, paraquat/diquat will soon burn off all existing growth and can be used again prior to planting on seedlings which subsequently spring up, without any ill effects on the soil.

These are places where weeds often get a foothold and multiply. Hedge bottoms in particular house ground elder, bindweed, couch-grass and other weeds with creeping rootstocks which are difficult to extract because of the roots of the hedge. Herbicides can be fatal to a hedge unless selected and applied very carefully and they should not be of the deeply penetrating soil-acting type like sodium chlorate. Dalapon can be carefully used to control couch so long as this is done before the hedge starts into growth in the spring. Applications of paraquat/diquat will destroy annual weeds and check the perennials if it is possible to apply without wetting the foliage of the hedge. The perennials will be dealt with more effectively by selective herbicides of the 2,4-D type, but again the herbicides must not come into contact with the hedge.

Climbing weeds like the larger bindweed scrambling over hedges and shrubs obviously cannot be treated with selective herbicides. An effective if somewhat tedious method is to carefully unwind or otherwise detach a few centimetres of the growing tips of the weeds and to dip them in a jam jar containing a strong solution of the herbicide, taking great care that they do not dangle and drip on to the leaves of the hedge. Such persistent painstaking treatment can greatly reduce and perhaps eliminate entirely these tenacious weeds.

Fences, particularly chain-link, can become very unkempt with grass and weeds at the base because of the difficulty of keeping on top of these by manual means. If no plants are growing there or within a foot or so of the fence, treatment with paraquat/diquat is fairly simple, but dichlobenil applied in the spring to a carefully controlled narrow strip is even more effective and should keep the fence line clear for a whole season. If the other side of the fence is neighbouring property, as much consideration should be given to the plants growing there, otherwise relations may become strained or claims for damages result.

Here one is free to use total weedkillers, provided that one is careful in their application and does not overlook the possibility of spread to plants growing on either side, more particularly with sodium chlorate which tends to creep sideways. Either simazine or dichlobenil applied in the spring will ensure weed-free paths for the rest of the year.

Dichlobenil is probably best for treating the crevices between paving, if these have not been grouted in and are sprouting weeds, for applied dry it can be sprinkled simply and economically along the crevices without being applied to the whole path. Alternatively, a cut-down dribble bar on a watering-can will enable liquid herbicide to be applied with the minimum of waste.

After treating a path it is important not to walk on it and then over the lawn while the herbicide is wet or while the granules are still on the surface, for serious damage to the turf may result.

As stated above, newly sown and turfed lawns should not be treated with the usual selective weedkillers for six months after sowing. If broad-leaved weeds put in an appearance, either ioxynil or morfamquat may be applied after the grass seedlings have made their second leaves.

Although lawn sand is still sold and used, it really has been ousted almost completely by the selective herbicides. It is however still quite effective against the flat, broad-leaved rosettes of daisies, dandelions and plantains. When using it, one must bear in mind that it may cause some temporary scorching of the grass followed by a surge in growth due to the nitrogen contained in the sulphate of ammonia; and that such feeding is not desirable in the latter part of the summer when, with winter in mind, one should be thinking in terms of phosphates and potash to balance the effects of nitrogen, to encourage root-growth and to stiffen up the grass.

In the description of the selective lawn herbicides, enough has been said to guide one's choice according to the nature of the weed problem. While these substances will give results throughout the growing season, they are usually most effective when the weeds are in their most active stage of growth from early May until the end of July. A dressing of summer fertiliser applied a week or so prior to treatment will stimulate the weeds and to further ensure plenty of receptive surface, ie leaf growth, the lawn should not have been mown less than two days before treatment. A still day, with little possibility of rain for several hours, should be chosen. Periods of drought and scorching sun are not the best times to make the application, for these conditions may result in scorching of the turf. A period of two or three days should then elapse before the grass is mown; and the mowings from this cut should not be placed on the compost heap. Always be ready to make a second application a month or six weeks later, particularly in the case of difficult weeds, if the first application has not been 100 per cent effective. It is better to hit these weeds again when they are reeling, than to give an extra heavy initial dose.

Pearlwort will seed even under close mowing; and with this weed I have found that one gets a more permanent control if much of the dead growth is raked out subsequently to encourage the seeds to germinate, when another application of herbicide can be given.

Timing this form of lawn weed-control is often the most exasperating part of the operation, for the chances of getting the right weather at the right time between mowings is probably rather less than fifty-fifty. This apart, with the right mixture and the correct rate of application, it is the surest way of obtaining and maintaining a weed-free lawn.

Moss in lawns is encouraged by bad drainage; surface panning and lack of aeration; and weak grass-growth through nutritional deficiencies. Putting these defects right must be the first consideration if one is to get the upper hand. Shady lawns are the most susceptible to invasion and here of course there may be little one can do to make the conditions less favourable.

Ordinary lawn sand with iron sulphate and sulphate of ammonia

L

as the active ingredients will give some measure of control, but it is more effective when mercurous chloride replaces the sulphate of ammonia. This mercurised lawn sand will kill the moss and some of the spores. Spring is the best time to make the application, and if much of the dead moss is raked out a week or so later, the grass will breathe again. The remaining moss spores will be encouraged to germinate and can then be dealt with. If the moss is in patches, care should be taken, when raking out, not to spread the material over moss-free areas, otherwise these will become infested with spores.

The newer chemical, chloroxuron, kills the moss by contact and then remains active in the soil for several months, taking care of any aftergrowth of moss without harming the grasses. It can be applied either in the spring or in autumn, and the ground must be moist at the time of application or rain expected. It should be used only on lawns which have been established for twelve months; and if any thickening of the grass is necessary after dense moss growth has been eradicated, a period of three months must elapse before grass seed is sown. A dressing of fertiliser to suit the season is desirable after any form of moss treatment, for this encourages the grass to form its own barrier against any reinfestation.

ROSE-BEDS AND BORDERS

Provided that the beds or borders are free of other plants, simazine applied at a low-dosage rate in the spring will control all annual weeds during the season if the ground is not disturbed afterwards. If needs be, paraquat/diquat can be applied very carefully first to kill any existing weeds. If perennial weeds are the problem and the roses have been planted for at least two years, dichlobenil applied in early February before bud-growth of the roses begins, has been proved safe except on very light soils.

FLOWER-BEDS AND BORDERS

Here herbicides can be used to only a limited extent. With beds which are planted twice a year, annual weeds tend to become established as the flowers fade and interest begins to wane. When the old plants are pulled out, the residue of weeds can be sprayed with paraquat/diquat before the beds are dug and replanted, which can be done safely twenty-four hours after the herbicide has been applied.

While in nursery circles much research is being done on the control by herbicides of weeds between herbaceous plants, there is still no really safe method that can be applied to the home gardener's herbaceous border. If it is an established one, while the ground is still clear of weeds in the spring, propachlor granules can be spread to keep the ground free of germinating weeds for six to eight weeks, by which time, if the border has been planted properly, the rightful occupants should be beginning to close in on any weeds which may germinate subsequently.

These few chemical aids apart, weed-control in flower-beds and borders usually resolves itself into the manual methods of hoeing and hand weeding, reduced to a minimum if my previous suggestions for planting to crowd out weeds have been followed.

SHRUBBERIES

Much the same treatment as for rose-beds can be carried out, again if no non-woody plants are present, unless these are confined to the frontage, when it may be possible to steer clear of them and still treat the bulk of the shrubbery. I must however issue a word of warning about dichlobenil, for it is not acceptable to all shrubs and ornamental trees. Any warnings on the containers as to susceptible species should be noted carefully. There is moreover still some divergence of opinion concerning its effect on certain subjects, and until the situation has been clarified completely, my advice is that if in doubt do not risk it, unless it be for the purpose of spot treating the occasional deep-rooted perennial weed.

ROCK-GARDENS

The programme here is simple for one is virtually back to the time-honoured method of hand weeding, doing this before the weeds have seeded. With a little care, perennial weeds which are entrenched so firmly between the stones that they cannot be extracted fully can be spot treated with a selective herbicide like 2,4-D, applied with a paint-brush to avoid splashing the rock-plants.

AMONG FRUIT-TREES AND BUSHES

Simazine, paraquat/diquat and dichlobenil, as recommended for roses, with similar precautions will keep the ground beneath clear of weeds for a whole season. If couch-grass is the main offender, it will be safe to use dalapon at a low dosage rate in November, or dichlobenil if wider control is required.

THE VEGETABLE GARDEN

In most respects this falls in line with flower-beds and borders: a clean start for planting or sowing, propachlor granules as a pre- and post-emergent herbicide to certain crops, and a limited amount of subsequent treatment with paraquat/diquat, although perhaps not quite so limited as for flowers, as the wider and rather more regular spacing of the plants enables this to be done more easily and with less chance of damage. As the crops close in, the hoe and the hand will then be necessary to keep on top of any weeds which have escaped early treatment or which have germinated subsequently.

So we come to the end of a rather long story. It began with plants in nature: species which have never found a place in our gardens because of their humble mien but which will not be denied in their unceasing efforts to ensure the existence of their kind; and in this survival of the fittest they are endowed with the ways and means of rapid reproduction and spread. What better for them than the fatter feeding-ground of the garden among the prima donnas and those plants which, perhaps through cultivation or because they are out of their natural environment, constitute less tough opposition than plants fighting for existence in the wild?

The story ended on the scientific means that man, frail man, has brought to his aid. How much he today depends on science to grow his crops. But I still say that the surest and the most satisfying way to win the battle against nature's trespassers is to deny them a foothold and to have properly planned defences manned by well-knit ranks of defenders: in other words, to plan, plant and cultivate with the suppression of weeds in mind. I can think of no more fitting epitaph than the words of Abraham Lincoln:

Die when I may, I want it said of me by those who knew me best that I always plucked a thistle and planted a flower where I thought a flower would grow.

GLOSSARY OF BOTANICAL TERMS

Adventitious roots Roots which arise from a stem.

Bi-generic A hybrid between two different genera.

Bract A modified leaf, sometimes green, sometimes coloured, sometimes scale-like, situated below a flower head or shoot or enclosing a single flower.

Capsule A several celled dry fruit which splits open when ripe.

Cultivar The term now adopted for garden variety.

Farina White meal on stems, leaves or flowers.

Floret A small flower, usually one of a cluster as the individual 'petals' of the daisy family.

Genus (pl *genera*) The term for a group of closely related species. The first part of a Latin name eg *Bellis perennis*, where *Bellis* is the genus and *perennis* the species.

Glaucous Covered with a bluish-grey or bluish-white bloom.

Herb A plant without a woody stem.

Hip or *hep* The fruit of the rose.

Hybrid A plant arising from a cross between two species.

Inflorescence The arrangement of flowers on a flower stem.

Lanceolate Lance-shaped.

Node The joint of a stem where leaves are attached.

Ovate Egg-shaped.

Palmate Lobed or divided in a palm or hand-like manner.

Panicle A branched raceme.

Pendent Hanging down, drooping.

Procumbent Trailing over the ground.

Prostrate Growing flat on the ground.

Raceme A simple elongated inflorescence, consisting of a single stem bearing single-stalked flowers along its length.

Radical leaves Leaves which arise from the roots or from a part of the stem at ground level.

Reticulated With network appearance.

Rhizome A swollen, creeping, underground stem, occasionally on the surface, as with bearded iris.

Rootstock A short, erect underground stem.

Runner A trailing shoot which roots and produces new plants at the nodes.

Spathe A single bract enclosing one or a number of flowers and often mistaken for a true flower eg arum lily

Species A group of individuals with similar characteristics which form a genus.

Spike An inflorescence, consisting of a number of stalkless flowers growing close together on an elongated unbranched stem.

Sport A shoot different in character from the parent plant, or in the flowers it produces. A new cultivar is sometimes raised from it.

Stolon A shoot which creeps just above or just below the ground and produces a new plant at its tip.

Sub-shrub A small shrub which tends to die down to the base each year.

Sucker A shoot which originates below ground and eventually appears above it, sometimes at some distance from the stem.

Taproot A main, usually central, descending root.

Trifoliate A leaf consisting of three leaflets arising from the same point.

Tuber A swollen part of a stem or root produced below the ground.

Variegated Leaves with usually yellow, whitish or silvery patches dispersed in the natural green.

Whorl Three or more leaves or flowers arising in a circle from a single node of the stem.

ACKNOWLEDGEMENTS

My sincere thanks are due to John Davison of the Weed Research Organisation and to Roy Lancaster for reading through the book; to Ceiba-Geigy for permission to use their Weed Tables to assist in the line drawings; to my son, Christopher, for the line drawings and to Elsa Megson, Bob Corbin and Ernest Crowson for providing the photographs.

INDEX